The Little Black Book

by Cadwallader and Nudnick

ILLUSTRATED BY R. TAYLOR

DOUBLEDAY & COMPANY, INC., GARDEN CITY, NEW YORK, 1957

The Little
Black Book

A MANUAL FOR BACHELORS

NOTE OF ACKNOWLEDGMENT

Because we have spent so much time in hotels, we have numbered the pages starting with 101. We also did this to increase the scope of the manual and to acknowledge that vast bulk of material that goes without saying.

Grudgingly dedicated to the two little girls without whose jeers and snide remarks this book would never have been finished.

Preface

This book is addressed to men, which should assure it of a high readership among that other sex. We have felt that a manual such as we present has long been overdue. Politics had its Machiavelli, who was willing to speak a few plain truths, but where among books is there a guide for bachelors? You hold the answer in your hand.

The reader may think it is presumptuous of anyone to write such a book, but he does not know C & N. Ours is not a "kiss & tell" record of accomplishment but is written from the deep knowledge that comes only with failure (not our own of course, but as a result of research and inquiry).

From locker rooms and bars, from smokers and lavatories, we have enlisted the best bachelor brains of our acquaintance; and, through keyhole and transom, we have gleaned the hitherto unwritten truths that abound in this slender volume, not only for your edification, reader dear, but for our own.

Women have had a franchise on romance since the Garden of Eden. They are the haves and you, boys, the have-nots. They bargain from strength. You may preen yourself on having the bat and ball, but they own the playground, and so hapless males ever since have had their eyes glued to the knotholes, tried to scale the fence and crash the gate, anything to avoid the prosaic turnstile of marriage. Our book shall be concerned with the contest itself and not the awarding of trophies.

Contents

The Little Black Book

1. About These Girls Now

Some philosopher once said that the proper study of mankind is man. Any modern bachelor knows better than that so, about these girls now. If the word "study" in the opener should give you to think that we are going to be stuffy and pedantic about our subject, you're in for a disappointment.

When we first decided to betray womankind by writing this book, there were three of us. Now we are but two, C & N[1]. X is no longer with us. Unlike ourselves, X was more interested in the True Nature of Woman than in her habits, seasons and general behavior. Instead of asking "Where?" he began by asking "What is a Woman?" And there he left us. We understand he ended up in a Trappist Monastery. He must have found out what he wanted to know.

Happily bereft of X's ridiculous viewpoint, we have proceeded in our own way. We have learned that woman should not be scrutinized but regarded superficially so as to perceive her best qualities. Realizing that it is ignorance, not knowl-

---

1 For reasons of convenience throughout this book, your writers shall refer to themselves as C & N. We found that in undertaking research for this manual that we of necessity became privy to the personal affairs of many interesting characters, male and female. Showing a disposition to listen patiently to this kind of talk, we soon acquired that affection

edge, which preserves illusion and generates enthusiasm, we shall hew to this line.

Before getting lost in a discussion of particular types of girls, we should like to examine Woman the concept. That Woman is a concept, as well as an actuality, is evident in the names we bestow on things. The bigger these things are the more certain they are to be designated as feminine: Mother Earth, for example. Since man is usually the giver of names, it may be because he considers ships, automobiles, and machines, in general, beautiful and expensive that he regards these as feminine. Show him an engraving of *Le Bonhomme Richard* and he will say: "She sure was a beauty." Even if he sights a whale, sex unknown, he unhesitatingly cries down from the rigging: "Thar she blows!" If the weather should be unduly warm, the day itself acquires sex as the filling-station attendant confides that: "She's a hot one today!" Exceptions have been attempted. Ask a man to enlist to serve *Der Vaterland* and he winds up fighting for his mother country.

It is now clear, boy, that no matter where you may be or what you may be doing, you're always thinking about women. In other words, a man has sex on his mind and a woman has it on her hands. As your brokers, in a manner

---

and confidence that is loosely bestowed on good listeners. It was not long before we were sought out by many romantic malcontents who wished to obtain help. So began our advice to the loveshorn bachelor.

At first we had no notion of profiting from these interviews, but as our fame increased, our time diminished until, alas, we were forced to establish the C & N Clinic and charge a nominal fee for consultations. It is well known that few people ever heed free advice, so having the true interest of our patients at heart, we reluctantly let them pick up the tab. We have drawn freely on our case-history files because we feel that the use of this material, intimate by its very nature, serves to enliven the text.

of speaking, we feel that you two should get together after a final admonishment or so.

At times throughout these pages we may make an appeal to the bachelor reader's better self. We do not direct this appeal to anything so flimsy as his sense of morals but namely to his sportsmanship. Few men would be offended if they were termed wicked, but call one of them a bad sport and you have hit him where he lives. Again and again we shall say, PLAY THE GAME!

MEN VS. WOMEN

No woman is an amateur if by "amateur" one would imply lack of knowledge or skill. All women are born with a veritable constellation of instincts that aids them without thinking. For this reason they are always ahead of you, but don't assume because you can't understand them that they are complex. Men fail to understand women precisely because they are more simple than men. In assuming that her pattern of thought is an intricate web, a man goes off on a tangent to become lost in the mystery of space while she blithely follows a *clear, straight line.*

Let perish the thought that she is romantic by nature. This is another error that she would encourage. The best argument we can advance that it is not women but men who are truly romantic is the fact that, for centuries, men have created all the music, painting, and poetry of any consequence. Unless you would bracket Carrie Jacobs Bond with Beethoven, Rosa Bonheur with Michelangelo, don't bother to try to refute this. We admit Elizabeth Barrett Browning embarrasses our argument, but, remember, she was a sick girl.

From the foregoing, you might assume that women have no inner life. We do not wish to go so far as that. The ques-

"A man who is privileged may . . . glance up from his watch and see a strange miracle occur."

tion of whether or not women have souls used to be a popular topic with medieval philosophers. But C & N are willing to concede here. We, for one[1], are practically convinced they do have souls.

But let us contemplate the difference between men and women in more intimate detail. One of the prime differences between man and woman is that man has habits and woman has rituals. Contrast your own quick shower, once-over with a razor, clean shirt, and the rubbing of the calf with each shoe with her ritualistic behavior as she moves in a kind of a trance. She is like an alchemist preparing to transmute base metal into shining gold. Around her are hot irons and ominous wind machines as well as countless substances: chemicals, greases, creams, jellies, liquids, powders, and colored pastes, all goops which have acquired their potency through repeated incantations said over them by voices on radio, television, and across counters. That the labels themselves have mystic powers is a possibility.

After her bath, which makes a scrubbing surgeon look like a small boy anxious to get back to a game of shinny, she emerges and begins. Enough sprays and powders fill the air to produce a prancing white horse on the Orpheum stage, but she has a larger purpose in view.

Apart from all the ingredients mentioned above, the main thing consumed is time. After an hour or so of strange grimaces followed by wandlike passes in the air above her head with a comb, the first act is concluded and she is ready to dress (which is all she said she was going to do in the first place). Now she ponders closets and shoe racks while she mutters in some cabalistic way. Finally the donning of the

---

1   See, dear. C.

raiment begins. With serpentine movements, squirming, straining, and tugging, she puts on a girdle. Next, the stockings and high heels. (A glimpse, at this moment, would convince the male onlooker that this batch, too, is going to turn out all right.) Then, slipping into her dress, she does a kind of minuet (school of Martha Graham) with her alter ego, the mirror. If she gets an approving nod from that carping partner in the glass, the dance is over and she presents herself.

The mystery and the miracle are impressive. Beginning with just an ordinary human being, she has, before our very eyes, created WOMAN.

Strangely enough, the highest accolade which can now be given her is for a man to snort, paw the Axminster, and say that he now has an uncontrollable urge to undo the glorious result. She receives this tribute irritably if the man chances to be her husband and replies in accordance with ancient tradition: "Not now, dear." (Only strangers and bachelors may have this privilege.) She will punish the husband for having married her by insidiously undoing the previously miracle later that night and presenting him with but a fraction of it, the lowest common denominator, *herself*, thereby preserving the mystery of that WOMAN that she keeps in bottles and closets. (Of course, some husbands don't care, feeling that undressing one's own wife is like taking down the Christmas tree—a sad business.)

The goings on just depicted could apply to any average, pretty girl making her toilette. When a woman reaches stature as an individual, acquires glamour and renown, the effect of the miracle is compounded and the wonder amplified as presses roar and people genuflect in the streets. Reams of chiffon, old lace, and newsprint are required to attire her in a manner appropriate to her magnitude. The pyramids could have been boxed up and sent to the Iowa State Fair with less ceremony and received less attention than the recent cumbersome job of transporting one slender American blonde to Monaco.

Now, who is the object of all this hullabaloo and pother that woman go through? The answer is YOU, bachelor chum, and, lands a Goshen, while time is with you, *take every advantage!* Insist on the whole enchilada, don't question the miracle or accept less than the entire package because, after all, divest Woman of all her trappings and what have you got? Yipes! SENSATIONAL!

CURTAIN GOING UP

First, dismiss the notion that all women are alike even with the lights out. We shall examine this fallacy on the level of the individual before going into comparisons of national differences. Rarely do you come upon a true strain or textbook picture like the following types, so please regard these classifications as merely a helpful index. In utilizing this material, you must practice rule of thumb because the possible combinations are infinite.

But now, Lights! Overture! Here they are, the little darlings! As a matter of form we follow the order of seniority, so first, we give you that most ancient of her kind. . . .

THE PRO

As bachelors, we feel this lady has her place in the world but it is not our world. Pursuit and conquest, that is, the thrill of the chase, have no meaning for her sort. Any man who patronizes her is on a par with the unlucky angler who buys his fish at the market after disappointment in deeper waters.

Any man who patronizes the Pro is on a par with the unlucky angler who buys his fish at the market.

We acknowledge a certain sneaking admiration for her forth-rightness in hawking her wares as she does, thereby making all other women seem coy.

INTELLECTUAL GIRL

Unless you happen to be a big brain yourself, you should make no effort to meet Athena on her own level. If she has been around a little while, she probably learned to conceal her high forehead from the cretins she has been dating. Any woman is less vain about her brain than her figure even if she is a Ph.D. So praise her curves and build her up till she feels like Marilyn Monroe. Ignore her diploma and treat her like a sweater girl[1] or she may become your Phi Bete Noir. Having canvassed hundreds of girls, we found that females in college indulge in intimate heterosexual relationship far more frequently than those in grade school, hence the inescapable conclusion that higher education is detrimental to conventional moral standards. We believe that C & N are the first to note this corollary.

LUSH

We shall dispense with her quickly. The Lush doesn't mind if she does, but presents the problem of making a Hollandaise sauce . . . in other words . . . getting her to the right point before she curdles. If John Barleycorn beats your time, accept it. Play the game and never shoot a sitting duck.

ATHLETIC TYPE

Many girls affect an interest in athletics in order to increase their scope and extend it to the daytime hours, or because they feel they look well in shorts or bathing suits. However,

---

1   A cashmere-bearing mammal with a high threshold of pleasure.

should you find yourself bivouacked with one of these vira-goes you may be in for an exhausting time of it. If her interest in sports extends to the boudoir, she may continue your humil-iation there as well as beating you five sets in the hot sun. Check in with your doctor before seriously pursuing one of these Dianas. Maybe what you really need is a hot-water bottle in bed.

FLIRT

A flirt is any girl who is reasonably courteous to another man in your presence. All girls are flirts, and be grateful for that or she might not have spoken to you in the first place. However, if she confines her activities to coquetry alone, then this means trouble and brings us to the attractive nuisance who conducts a one-woman war against men possibly due to some slight, real or imaginary, occurring sometime between the playpen and the nursery school. She has dedicated her-self to your frustration for she is the Tease, a direct lineal descendant of the Siren, so plug your ears and stay off the reefs. No two ways about it, this personable wench should really be fenced and posted for all to heed. It is hard to resist the challenge she offers, but you will finally learn the secret of her fascination is that she is as insincere as you are. Dirty pool! Like the one that got away, you will remember her when the others are forgotten. For those who value the game as much as the reward, C & N say try your luck but don't say we didn't warn you. Should you, by any gaudy chance, suc-ceed, get in touch. We would like to spend an afternoon tying flies with you.

CAREER GIRL

A career girl is a problem to you and herself. She is the donkey

*Ignore her diploma and treat her like a sweater girl
or she may become your Phi Bête Noire.*

between two stacks of hay. In addition to the usual routine of courting, your conversation must be liberally larded with promises of opportunities relevant to her ambitions. You must either have connections or be a liar to appeal to her. To long maintain such a liaison, some concrete results must be forthcoming or she's off like a bird. Most of the younger career girls have a wholesome attitude toward marriage; they are just not interested.

Rarely is a girl in this category interested in you as a person. However, there is always one subject of keen mutual interest which will command her fascinated attention, namely, herself. So, like a good golfer, keep your head down, eye on the ball, and follow through.

The career girl who has definitely arrived may feel she can consider a man for himself. He can do her no favors but she may grant him hers. She is no longer as selfish as she was because now she has everything except you, you lucky dog. She will love you with the full intensity of half her whole being for all eternity. That is to say, for six months, or as long as you can bear it.

JAIL BAIT

One forgets that the symbol of the romantic female, Juliet, no less, was really jail bait, being a scant fourteen at the time she and Romeo were an item. This fresh stuff is for those who would sacrifice a bit of seasoning for the tenderness of the morsel itself. She is the peculiar prey of the fatherly type who, in his kindly desire to educate her, proceeds to subject her to the very things he would caution her against. We say, be patient—kill time rather than do time. Soon she will be a mature woman of eighteen.

GOLD DIGGER

This one knows the price of everything and the value of nothing being done without payment in advance. A bachelor of average means confronted by this sort finds himself in a stalemate situation. Each has what the other wants. Simple barter is in order here but, against your short funds, she has unlimited natural resources. You may try a marginal operation for a time here, but she will sell you short the first time you fail to cover. Unlike the pro, this prospector does not make the mistake of operating on too small a scale and so escapes the stigma the other accepts and endures. The G.D. regards love as big business and she knows her business. She can tell whether you are paste or real at twenty paces and measures the B.T.U.s in the warmth of her greeting at so much per karat. The purest example of her ilk to come to our attention is a jewel-encrusted dame we know who celebrates New Year's Eve on June 30th, the end of the fiscal year.

ONE OF THE BOYS

Some girls are just what the caption indicates, while other misguided ones aspire to this category and are chagrined when accepted on this basis. A passion for eavesdropping on men-talk sometimes spurs the very young to achieve this dubious position. A desire to be consistent makes them easy marks like the stool pigeons they are. A truly smart feminine dish never seeks to diminish the advantage of being different from the boys.

NYMPHO

The nymphomaniac can best be defined as someone who likes something at least as well as you do. The problem here is one of recognition. This may take time, say forty-five minutes, but

One of the boys.

from then on it is the old question of fighting a wildcat, how to let go and keep face. In the case of this hamadryad, a subtle approach is about as necessary as using a beagle hound in a shooting gallery. She'll ask you and here your aye will be bigger than your stomach for this task. You'll find it rather like trying to keep a ninety-pound tuna in the bottom of the boat.

GIRL FRIEND

This individual is not a true type; she has no identity of her own. In the theater of romance, she is a faceless spear carrier. She is parasitically attached to any one of the other archtidbits listed here. Sometimes, generally late at night after the administering of sufficient alcohol, she begins to materialize and may even seem desirable, but in the morning this illusion dissolves. The girl friend is an impediment to progress, a kind of modern duenna. The most attractive thing about her is her prettier companion, whom you have as little chance of seeing alone as you have of seeing *Pagliacci* without *Cavalleria Rusticana*. Oddly enough, her charm and appeal may be evident to other men but never to you . . . and she has a most annoying habit of intermittently bestowing herself upon the unlucky as a Consolation Prize.

THE LADY

The term persists in a form of address (Ladies and Gentlemen) as a plural of which the singular is unknown as in "news." And who is responsible? Why, the Lady herself! She was last seen some years ago jumping into men's trousers, grabbing a lunch box, and rushing for the streetcar with a career glint in her eye, and she hasn't been heard from since. Naturally when the female of a species ceases to exist, her male counterpart, the gentleman, of necessity disappears, having no longer anyone to whom he may address himself. We regret there is no lady in this book.

OF VIRGINS

In deference to the superstitious among our readers, we will treat of virgins of whom so much has been written in legend and mythology. (We speak of full-grown virgins.) Mind you, we do not deny categorically that such creatures exist; rumors reach our desk constantly; only recently one was reported near Chicago but by an unreliable observer.

Virginity is a condition found in the very young, not unlike the "soft spot" on the head of a baby. It is really nothing to worry about for it usually goes away by itself before the child is very old. If it lingers, virginity proves embarrassing to its possessor as well as her family and friends. Like a lisp, it's cute up to a point.

Identification is difficult. A vine-ripened beauty is reluctant to admit she is one but is indignant if you assume she isn't. She doesn't know whether to feel proud or unwanted. It's all very confusing. You might as well follow the advice in Jail Bait and when you bring them up to the boat and find they're below the legal limit, toss them back like a veteran angler.

FOREIGN BODIES

China Doll: NOW DON'T ASK US! We've never been there. But we understand that, in her ancient land, they view sex with greater latitude than we Occidentals, so we feel China offers new horizons to be explored by the migratory bachelor.

Italian Girl: The modern Mona Lisa comes in a wide assortment of colors and sizes. Creeping up the thigh of the Italian boot toward the mountains, we frequently encountered blonde hair as well as brunette. Of equal interest to the tourist is the fact that the native land of Boccaccio and Casanova contributes to the decline and fall of the Roman vampire as regularly as clockwork by sweeping the womenfolk from the streets into darkened interiors through the simple device of closing all shops between 1 and 4 P.M. daily. This is known as the siesta. Now, we ask you, compare *that* with your own measly fifteen-minute coffee break!

Redcoat: The English Miss is noted for her complexion which does not stop at the neck (most of the taller Parisian show girls are British). Beneath this smooth insulation are some pretty scalding contents, and a little investigation will reveal that Jane Eyre and Moll Flanders are sisters under the skin. Her haughty manner may put you off but, while you are stammering about a visit to the Tate, she may come out flat-footed, in accents clipped and brittle, and suggest something a little more bracing, by Jove!

Danish Pastry: After a kermess or two in Denmark, we will grant that these Danish cupcakes are an attractive, warm-hearted, generous lot but, like the Swedes and Norwegians, they are so damn wholesome and aboveboard about *every-thing* that we hardly stayed a month. Such hospitality! We left with a sheepish feeling that reminded us of an afternoon in our childhood when we spent hours digging a hole under the center-field fence only to find when we got in that all kids were admitted free—never really enjoyed the game even though the home team won.

Comrade: Forgetting the royal example of Catherine the Great, who made everything, including history, in the boudoir, the modern Russian woman chooses to show her prowess in the shot-put ring. She is hard to approach as an individual because she generally travels in squads, platoons, or brigades, marching in lock step. But, placing our faith in biology and not to be deceived by a sweat shirt, we say, "Come on out, Ninotchka—we know you're in there."

Vive La France: In our travels we have had the opportunity to observe the French girl at firsthand and could not help but compare her to her obstreperous American cousin. The Gallic belle is affectionate, devoted to man's pleasure, and dedicated to the sound notion that he is the most important thing in life. She is eager to please but retains her fascination and mystery, is well-groomed, yet, above all, is exceedingly feminine. She is, in a word, a WOMAN, and this within minutes after reaching puberty, and from then on she never forgets this simple, all-important fact. The only picayunish drawback to her otherwise flawless, petite charm is the fact that she has wide feet.

And the American Girl?: The American is notoriously spoiled and, outside of an attractive façade and figure from head to toe, lacks all the vital assets which are the natural attributes of her Parisian rival, but, nevertheless—we'll take the American girl every time we can! After all, who wants wide feet?

We feel that if a man can master Miss America, all other women in the world present no real problem. A man who can bust a bronco is a proven horseman; all that remains is simple equitation with more tractable mounts.

The rest of this book shall largely concern itself with the care and feeding of the American girl. There are certain ways and means to be employed by the knowing bachelor. We shall discuss them in logical order.

2. How to Meet Girls

Statisticians maintain that for every man (represented by 1.00) in the U. S. there are 1.03 women. This .03 bit of lagniappe is not to be sneered at; it totes up to a margin of some two million or so, forming a pool of romantically unemployed females that is almost enough to make us understaffed bachelors quail at the prospect, and the prospect of quail is no light matter.

In face of this veritable horde of spare parts, the problem of meeting girls should be easy—and so it is. But one thing to keep in mind is that our standards of etiquette date back to a time when women were more scarce in our frontier nation and tradition still dictates the necessity of a proper introduction, lacking, as it may, the formality required in Grandma's day. The most notable forward step taken since then is that now the background, character, and reputation of the introducer is of no importance whatsoever. Today anyone, with no more credentials than a felon on parole (your bookie, for instance), can perform this office by simply saying, "Brunhilde, meet my buddy Siegfried," and a light kindles in her eyes and the fat is in the fire.

(Or alternately—"Pocahontas, drop that load of kindling and meet Captain Smith.")

*Check in with your doctor before seriously pursuing
one of these Dianas.*

Another marked advance in social protocol is that the character of the man *being* introduced is no longer even relevant. Every American girl has heard the phrase, "Don't speak to any strange men," dinned into her ears so often since she was a child that even the loneliest, love-starved chick is apt to turn on her heel when approached by a stranger. It is not that she questions the moral rectitude of the man but simply that she *does not know his name.* Now, if only some third party steps up and says, "Emily, this is Jack Ripper," she becomes all smiles and her foolish juvenile fears vanish.

The time and place of the initial meeting is still as important as ever, but not because of social convention. Ideally, it should occur when and where you have circumstances under your control so that you can follow up any advantage that may occur. Granted, this is not always possible, but if you get off your francis and get around a bit, you'll be surprised at the number of women moving freely about unmolested—and here is where you come in. Women are often to be found in the most prosaic places; supermarkets, department stores, pharmacies, etc. How does one grasp opportunity without risking rebuff or worse?

Using the supermarket for example, a trespasser like yourself might do this: Having spotted some desirable wench in the fruit and vegetable section, start feeling a honeydew melon in a tentative manner. Then, as if talking to yourself, ask, "How can you tell when they are ripe?" and, with a helpless look, catch her eye. In matters domestic, women delight in showing superiority so, in this case, she will confidently take the melon, pressing the ends firmly with her thumbs while you double-check her fingers for a wedding ring. Thank her warmly, continue the conversation casually at the meat counter as she helps you select the best cuts; naturally you will carry her groceries to the car. If she drives off without giving you her phone number, you still have her name and address which surely you cadged off her registration slip on the steering column.

Now don't waste all your afternoons hanging around markets sullying fruit just because it worked so well that time. There are still such obvious catchalls as bars and restaurants where, if you need our help, you're hopeless. Airplanes and trains are a little more of a challenge but only for the novice. However, save yourself the bother of courting the smiling airline hostess who is secretly married to the pilot anyway.

Should you find yourself alone in a strange town of decent size, you can visit certain establishments where the girl, because of the nature of her employment, speaks to you first—salesgirls in general and rumba instructors in particular. Chances are good here but even more so if you can affect a Texas drawl as unctuous as an oil well. What might offend in a matter-of-fact northern twang comes out as a compliment in a lazy southern accent.

The offbeat aura of the art museum provides a romantic setting for the beginning of a beautiful friendship. An artist we know, who spends most of his time vainly searching for some girl named Jennie, admitted he found consolation by using the ensuing bilk: Breathing quietly, stand directly behind some delightful creature as she gazes at a *large* picture. When she steps back for a better view and bumps into you, steady her as you apologize, inquire if she is all right—not feeling faint perhaps—and offer to fetch her a drink of water. When she says no, suggest a martini possibly. If she smiles ever so little, make a sweeping gesture at the splendor of the walls laden with those El Grecos and Goyas and say: "Come, let me take you away from all this." And she just might.

Lonely hearts clubs are taboo. If you are despondent enough to go to one of these white-elephant dansants, you'll probably wind up with some misfit no better than yourself, and surely you wouldn't like that. We didn't.

THE COCKTAIL PARTY

Cocktail parties clearly afford the best opportunity to get acquainted with new girls, so let's have a party. You both look your best, introductions are routine, and she is constrained by ordinary courtesy to be pleasant. Not only has liquor lubricated your tongues and greased the skids under the inhibitions, but the greater part of the evening is still before you. If she is unescorted, the idea is to sneak up from down wind and scoop her off for dinner. True, you may fail to capture the body, but an introduction, though somewhat short of a writ of habeas corpus, does give you the opening for snaggling that sufficient minimum, her phone number.

In order to obtain those useful little digits, you must avoid being too sly or devious because girls arch their backs at transparent and petty deceits. Don't take the long way around the barn. Come right out and ask her politely, "May I call you sometime?" Never ask, "What is your phone number?" before obtaining the answer to the previous request. Such procedure may provoke a quick comeuppance. Another virtue of the more genteel approach is that, if she grants your wish by giving you her correct number, she has indicated her interest, which gives you a leg up, in a manner of speaking.

Naturally you will give her a buzz as soon as possible because there were other attractive men with similar ideas at that party. She will have had ample time to have forgotten you if many days elapse. There is nothing so embarrassing as hearing a chilly "Who?" after you have called and given your name. Explanations as to one's identity are always lame and feeble and she has you one down at the very outset. To avoid this mishap you could have used the C & N MEMORABLE REMARK, that is, the use of some outlandish, flattering, or absurd statement which must stick in her mind and give you a favorable tail wind. Almost immediately after being presented to this *average* pretty girl, you might have said any one of these ear catchers:

Have you ever shot the Colorado rapids in a soya-bean canoe?
I certainly want to wish you a lot of luck tomorrow night.
(When she expresses surprise by saying she's not doing anything tomorrow night, it's your cue to suggest dinner.)
Let's just keep it a quiet affair—only the immediate family.

The impudence of the above may make her laff. This is important; who wants to go all through life one evening with a girl without a sense of humor? Sharing laughter with her creates a feeling of intimacy equaled only by a kiss and even makes that easier. If one of our foregoing katzenjammers, coupled with the charm of your person, does not make an indelible impression on her, then our names are not Cadwallader and Nudnick.

3. The Telephone

We feel that the telephone deserves special attention in itself. It is not called a cradle phone for nothing; it can get you in a whole lot of trouble. This black tyrant is, at one and the same time, an instrument for pursuit and escape. It infinitely extends the field of operations and, in the conflict of the sexes, communications is as important as logistics. It is as indispensable to a bachelor as his automobile. Just as everyone is not a good driver, neither is he necessarily adept in the use of Alex G. Bell's device. In the interest of clarity and brevity, we enumerate the following points to keep in mind:

1. Have an exchange service. This will help to keep the date book full and gives you the option of rejecting or deferring unwanted calls.
2. Keep pencil, pad, cigarettes, ash tray, and calendar handy. Make notes and so avoid confusion.
3. Establish the fact (true or not) that you have a party line. This will account for busy signals on your line when you are playing possum.
4. Speak low. Develop a soft, well-modulated voice with intimate overtones. This can engender a favorable or receptive frame of mind in the female listener.

5. Artful dodges for terminating or avoiding conversation:

    a. Have buzzer at hand that sounds like your doorbell.

    b. Click telephone yourself and say that the operator must be trying to get through with an urgent call.

    c. Say you are expecting a long-distance call.

    d. Suggest phone is tapped. This is particularly effective in discouraging the married girls.

    e. Keep pets—real or imaginary. To say: "Pardon me, dear, but my hound just ran through the room with the parrot in his mouth"—usually suffices for an excuse to hang up.

    f. Answer in your best Japanese houseboy dialect —even if you are found out she may still think you are a card.

    g. Use the old stand-by of asking eagerly, "where are you, dear? I'll call you right back."

Don't become a creature of habit and constantly employ only one or two of the above ruses. Mix them up to avoid monotony and detection.

The telephone can be used either to make or receive calls. This is obvious, but we remind you of this simple fact because, in placing calls yourself, you control the situation, while in receiving them you might be at a disadvantage. When you make the call you can compose yourself, order your thoughts, consider your dialogue, and, most important, choose your time. When you think of the inopportune, even embarrassing, moments when the jangling bell can summon you unprepared, the clear advantage of retaining the initiative should be apparent.

"...embarrassing moments when the jangling bell
can summon you unprepared."

There is no way to forestall all unforeseen calls, but frequently, by previous arrangement, you can know when to
expect certain ones. When you are taken unawares you may,
in panic, resort to the truth, being at a loss for words, and find
yourself accepting a date that otherwise would be charmingly
deferred. The telephone can intrude not only on situations
but on your mood. Some of us are bright in the morning hours
while others need a rolling start. These latter fag enders might
as well leave the phone off the hook until noon.

Lee B., bachelor cum laude, observes strict protocol in his
use of the instrument. Before placing any calls to the opposite
sex, he is careful to be smooth-shaven, faultlessly garbed,
whether in sack suit or dressing gown, and even his shoes
must be shined. Obviously his appearance and attire is not
visible to the lady in question, but he is convinced that a
certain confidence and assurance which he feels, is com-
municated to his listener. So sensitive is he to the effect of
clothing and accessories that an Ascot tie can inspire a brilliant series of epigrams which would be unthinkable in bags
and sneakers. If a call is particularly important to him and the
impression to be made vital to his interest, Lee will dress for
the call as he would if the recipient were present.

He is particularly fastidious when talking to maitre d's
of certain well-known establishments. Realizing that these
gentlemen are the greatest of snobs, he has admitted to tying
and retying a Windsor knot four times until the foulard
dimpled in just the right manner. Then, and only then, did
he feel that he could have the proper jaunty tone in his voice
to commandeer a choice table. ·

You, reader dear, may be sickened by such sybaritical per-
fectionism as represented by Lee B., but, psychologists will
confirm that the underlying principle is sound. If you don't

believe it, just call little Miss No. 1 in your stable before you have brushed your teeth, and while wearing only the tops of your pajamas, and see if the old badinage is not a bit lame.

LITTLE BLACK BOOK

A telephone can be quite useless unless the bachelor has a Little Black Book in his possession at all times. We feel that its use is imperative. If you can remember a girl's number, it is an indication that you are seeing too much of her. The book will constantly surprise you with alternatives that you might otherwise forget.

The rudimentary kind of L.B.B. that a tenderfoot bachelor keeps merely contains names, addresses, and phone numbers. Acknowledging this to be the most vital information, we can hardly regard it as complete. For any worth-while chick at least a page should be reserved, with these suggested headings.

NAME
REAL NAME
PET NAME
ADDRESS
PHONE NO.
PARTY LINE
PRIVATE
RESIDES: ALONE
GIRL FRIEND
FAMILY
AGE
ACTUAL AGE
BIRTH DATE
HEIGHT
HEIGHT IN HEELS
WEIGHT

WAIST	BUST		HIPS
BROTHER'S FIGHTING WEIGHT		AGE	DISPOSITION

COLOR OF EYES	COLOR OF HAIR	TRUE COLOR OF HAIR
STOCKING SIZE	SHOE SIZE	INSEAM MEASUREMENT
FAVORITE FLOWER		FAVORITE MUSIC
FAVORITE DRINK		FAVORITE FOOD
FAVORITE SEMIPRECIOUS GEM		FAVORITE DRIVE-IN
LAST TIME YOU DATED HER		WHERE
YES		NO
REMARKS		

It is not practicable or wise to carry a volume of the dimensions necessary to record as much information as we have suggested. We advise that there be a Master Black Book kept in some safe place and a plebeian one for the pocket containing simply names and numbers for emergencies. We do not pretend that the form we have submitted is exhaustive; the resourceful bachelor will no doubt find numerous omissions which he can remedy. Our own personal form is far more intricate but still cannot compete with one we know which makes us feel truly humble.

One David M., prior to his recent marriage, used to maintain a filing system so complete as to be the wonder and envy of the few intimates who knew of its existence. He dubbed it THE PARI-MUTUEL INTEREST CALCULATOR OR P.I.C. He had been pursuing an entirely new field of cybernetics . . . a combining of his data with an electronic setup that not only computed sure things but dealt in an exhilarating manner with probabilities . . . fed the proper and relevant material, of course.

We would expect few dossiers to be as elaborate as those of Mr. M., but certain significant information about the fillies that one dates can be helpful; and, when we think of the possibilities of pooling these facts . . . well, sir! But to return to our boy, his *modus operandi* was delightfully simple. At the first sign of the sniffles or some minor affliction he would, with tender concern, dispatch his current cutie to his doctor who would take an exhaustive case history and give her a thorough physical examination. Since the doctor in question was a charlatan, as well as a member of his golf club, the above findings were available to M. With this as a beginning, he carried on until the complete file was a model of comprehensive Pinkerton research.

GLAMOROUS NEGLECT

Strategic use of the phone, when a girl is hot for you, can give her the illusion of being courted and getting attention without much wear and tear on the old retreads and bank account. With the help of an understanding sister, or girl pal, who can be schooled in the ways of a long-distance operator, you can give the impression of being a glamorous and well-traveled fellow by using the C & N long-distance gambit. The best exponent of this method is Ellsworth P.

It was our pleasure to see Ellsworth in actual operation. We had heard of his early success at simulating Paris, London, Madrid, and other capitals of the world. His young sister, indispensable ally, who served as operator, was now boning up on various patois and dialects and was warming to the task herself. She was eager to try Novgorod, U.S.S.R., but Ellsworth's Republican leanings forbade this. They finally compromised on Nairobi, in spite of his dislike of intense heat.

On the evening of which we speak, however, Ellsworth presented truly a magnum opus, a ship-to-shore conversation from the *Coronia* on the high seas. Ellsworth, although he had never been farther east than Blythe, California, eschewed the larger vessels like a seasoned traveler. For this particular conversation he had presumed on a Hollywood bit player of Cockney parts, who owed him five dollars, to handle the preliminaries. The sound effects were masterly: a continually

A ship-to-shore conversation from the Caronia *on the high seas.*

flushing toilet, a record faintly playing "Nearer, My God, To Thee" (which we thought a trifle morbid though effective), and some kind of ship's bell, which some unknown person sounded in the kitchen at intervals. The rotary motion Ellsworth used on the phone itself, moving it first near and then far from his mouth to imitate the rise and fall of volume on connections such as these, was a thing of beauty, but, best of all, was the genuine disbelief he showed at actually being able to hear the girl's voice on the other end. The eagerness and feeling he put into "Can you hear me, darling?" was unforgettable. We later admitted to each other that, even standing right there, we felt a wee bit seasick. The fact that the next day the local newspapers carried an item that the *Coronia* had been tied up by a longshoremen's strike in no way diminished the artistic merit of this great performance.

For those who are stirred by Ellsworth's example we say: begin modestly, be accurate about details, subscribe to the *National Geographic*, and haunt the travel bureaus. We must warn that the girl may take advantage of your "absence" to cut a few capers of her own.

4. The Automobile

A bachelor's automobile is more than a mere conveyance; it is a way of life. Today more men own cars than own homes, so now it may properly be said that a man's car is his castle. Granted that a Rolls-Royce is exceeded in most girls' estimation only by a Brink truck, there are other respectable alternatives from which to choose. If you can't pop for a Continental or a Cadillac, it is sometimes smart not to drop down just a notch or two in horsepower, but to go all the way to that snappy, modest-priced kind that can be called cute and has the aura of a second car. Only if you are a man of celebrated wealth can you afford to drive a seedy businessman's coupé, or what appears to be a company car.

Apart from your person, the impression that your car makes is one of the first things by which you will be judged. Be as tidy about your car as you are about yourself. Just as you would keep your nails clean, see that the windshield is clear at all times. Whitewall tires (a must) are like letting a judicious amount of shirt cuff show at your coat sleeves.

The younger girls are easily dazzled by the flashy convertible with extras: Bermuda carriage bells, twin pipes, etc. (a radio we regard as necessary as a carburetor). The slightly older girls (and that's old enough) have had their coiffures blasted to fright wigs often enough to prefer comfort to being conspicuous, so if you drive a convertible, keep the top *and* the payments up.

Willis C. is a great believer in the importance of the automobile in wooing. One day he called our attention to the fact that statistics prove that more proposals are made in the darkened interior of this portable vestibule, with its remarkable acoustics, than in any other one place. These need not be proposals of marriage, he hastened to remind us. Taken with his argument, as well as his Old Jack Daniel's, we pressed him to go on that we might glean a few interesting ideas, which forthcame.

The glove compartment, felt Willis, should not be a repository containing such necessaries as: old traffic-violation receipts, loser's tickets from Santa Anita, a sour half-eaten Hershey bar, a discarded windshield wiper, and a pair of greasy pliers (the standard equipment carried by the average provident male driver), but should show, from its contents, some foresight and imagination. He went on to say that there are certain little niceties that please women; and, without going so far as to make it a complete notion counter, the handy cubicle might contain the following articles: cold cream, Kleenex, chewing gum, mascara, Band-aids, a rattail comb, bobby and safety pins, a shoehorn, emory boards, and a Phillips screw driver. A vanity mirror on the sun visor, he confided, is mandatory.

As an encore thrown in with the above advice, Willis volunteered what he calls the "Care-to-drive?" operation. If one is satisfied that the girl can handle the car properly, then suggest that she take the wheel. He found that most young girls enjoyed the vote of confidence, and frequently took him up on it. He said that he never felt so devil-may-care as when he lounged in the luxury of seeing an eager young thing playing chauffeur to him . . . quite different from the helpless, subordinate feeling of being a passenger in her car. And, note this, since no one likes to drive aimlessly for very long, he would suggest, after a short while, that they stop at his apartment for a drink. This always worked. Since she was driving, she felt more like a creature of free will and less like a lamb being led, as she pulled up at his place, relaxed and open-minded.

In addition to the subtle fare served up by Willis, we should like to add a few prosaic turnovers of our own: Try to use your own car at all times. Don't be caught on a double date without your own transportation because of the obvious limitations that it imposes on your activities. (We hardly need expand on this.) Your skill, or lack of it, in handling a car will affect her. Give her a smooth ride, avoid unnecessary speed that might create anxiety or tension, and do a deft job of parking. If she finds you mechanically inept at the wheel, she may think your lack of co-ordination extends further.

The sports car, while appealing to some girls, nevertheless has certain obvious disadvantages. Nylons are strained to the running point and taffeta crushed and wrinkled as she squeezes in or out of that fancy little Whited Sepulcher that you borrowed for the night to impress her. Most of these little buggies require lots of handling with conventional four speeds forward and constant shifting; so, as a result, the only thing you can take into your hands is her life. And don't forget, in the privacy of the average car you can make lateral as well as forward progress.

Whereas such buggies as the Sekshul D V-8, the High

"Don't be caught on a double date without your own transportation."

Dudgeon, the Blue Funk are much in vogue at present, we feel that the sports-car fad will wane when American know-how succeeds in the mass production of a cheap, uncomfortable little car.

If, in spite of the disadvantages we have listed, your lady of the moment is incorrigibly addicted to these miniature nuisances, then we suggest you employ the following on this earthbound Jackie Cochran.

The FOREIGN CAR BIT is a relatively new caper. Though you have neither a foreign car nor the means to buy one, take her with you while you haunt the showrooms of these diminutive imported dandies and make the idea of purchase seem imminent. As you admire the sleek lines of a British Pimm's No. 1, tell the salesman that you have a whale of a deal going on an Italian Cinzano, not to mention a lead on a custom-made Waterfill-Frazier. Disdain the little and comparatively cheap N.G. which is too common now and is really nothing more than a motorcycle with its safety factors aroused. Next to mink itself, the European sports car is the badge of inspired indolence among the girls, and, as the Chinese say, "She who rides a Jaguar cannot dismount."

5. The Restaurant

A girl may not sell herself for a mess of potage, but, if it's cold vichyssoise in the right setting, she may become a hot prospect. Women regard the merit of the place where you dine as an index of your regard for her. The quality of the restaurants should diminish as an affair progresses. This can be accomplished subtly under the "adventures in fine eating" heading, if the man has his wits about him. Seldom should he make the mistake of asking the girl where she would like to go. In the average city there are usually about three answers, all expensive. Sometimes she may suggest a modest restaurant, but this has sinister undertones of "O Promise Me." It's up to the man to present his choice for the evening with a certain enthusiasm as if it were a planned surprise. A little epicurean chatter thrown in strategically can make a second-rate bistro bloom.

One of your main concerns in the average restaurant will be the manipulation of the menu. Here it is a case of à la carte vs. table d'hôte. Unless she actually wants only a salad or a sandwich, the idea is to stress the table d'hôte side of the menu. Smack your lips as you praise the *Boeuf Bourgignonne* (beef stew) as a dish which really tries the knowledge of both chef and epicure; any fool can broil a steak; it's the sauce and preparation that marks the great dishes. However, if she outsmarts you and insists on a Kansas City tidbit with *Sauce Bernaise* (85c extra), accept this move with smiling resignation, order spaghetti for yourself, and to hell with the wine. Console yourself that you left your coat in the car and who wears a hat?

Headwaiters present a special problem. To be respectfully addressed by one of them using your surname often impresses the girl. This applies only to the better restaurants and night clubs. If you are not a habitué of such, and we presume you are not, a small bribe when you make the reservation with your afternoon cocktail will accomplish this. Be just as careful, moreover, to cover yourself at the crummy dives you *usually* frequent so that the maître d' doesn't seem too chummy.

Another effective bit is the prearranged request for the girl (?) to produce her driver's license when being served a cocktail. This works better on women who are trying to forget their thirtieth birthday. Do not overplay this because there is the danger that she may wonder why she is out with a balding bastard like you.

C & N BLUE-PLATE SPECIAL

A man appreciates a well-dressed woman. The broad effect is for him, but the details and real finesse of her gown are for prying female eyes. A woman may undress for a man but she dresses for other women. Unfortunately the best place for her to be seen, by those who will envy or condemn, is in the better restaurants.

Much as the darlings love to go to "21" or Le Pavillon, a pair of Percherons, badly out of sorts, couldn't drag them in if their hair is not done nicely or if they are wearing the wrong clothes. Female vanity is the vulnerable spot that the world-wary bachelor goes to work on. If she doesn't look like a centaur in them he will encourage her to wear *slacks*, perhaps telling her that, of all women, only she and Marlene look really well in trousers. Trading on the fact that the finest restaurants frown on, if not forbid, women in slacks, a bachelor with a modicum of aplomb can even go so far as to actually pull up in front of an elite eating establishment, and then let *her* persuade *him* to go to a modest hamburger joint.

EPICUREAN CHEAT

Among our friends, Alfred B. is the most adept in the use of the Epicurean Cheat, that is, pretending to deride the plush places by *complaining* of the food. He has been known to protest that ————'s is vastly overrated, and that he would not be caught dead in a joint that passes off a slice of ripe olive as *truffe* on top of Eggs Benedict. He does this so vehemently that his righteous indignation infects the girl, and she does not question when he takes her elsewhere. He also uses the disdainful "We have had that, haven't we?" reference, apropos of certain de luxe food emporiums. This makes the young woman wish to rise to his blasé level by agreeing with him and consenting to a snack in a drive-in.

AQUA FRESCA, VINO PURO

Wine has the peculiar virtue of being the one drink that can be taken with any kind of meal. It not only enhances the food but preserves that glow so painstakingly acquired earlier in the evening. The soporific effect of eating is dispelled by this heavenly nectar, and, when followed by brandy, in the congenial form of a stinger, it's like Gehrig after Ruth . . . somebody is apt to score.

". . . cover yourself at the crummy restaurants you usually frequent . . ."

This remarkable stuff comes in all shades and colors suitable to anyone's taste, in hot weather or cold. True, it does up the tab a notch, but count chickens, not pennies. The act of ordering wine lends grace to the meal. The flourish with which the sommelier presents the wine list for your consideration gives you a momentary importance in her eyes. If you can follow through with a little knowledgeable gup about vintage, bouquet, etc., she may be impressed. The very names, Château Margaux . . . Romanee Conti . . . Vouvray . . . Lacrima Cristi (pronounced properly, of course), sound romantic and increase your stature, particularly with the neophyte. After examining the foreign products, suddenly discover an inexpensive California Napa Valley vintage which exceeds them all; she may not know better. Your cosmopolitan air can be confirmed in her opinion if, for some reason or other, you should rummage in your wallet and encounter a French franc note or a few Italian lire and say, "How did these get in here?" casually, natch. (These notes can be easily obtained at any stamp or coin shop, or, who knows, you may have actually been to Europe.)

And, in conclusion, don't forget that the old bubbly champagne is a wine . . . perhaps the most festive of all. The popping of the cork, the tickling sparkle, as well as its heady effect, has countless times made less tedious the journey to Paradise for many a weary bachelor.

6. The Bachelor's Apartment

The center court at Wimbledon, Madison Square Garden, the bull ring at Sevilla, all celebrated in sporting annals, are hardly as exciting scenes of action as the average bachelor's apartment.

But, before elaborating on the apartment itself, we should like to present a few suggestions.

GETTING HER TO YOUR APARTMENT

At no time should you make your apartment seem like a snare, but rather give it the aura of Forbidden Fruit. She will scarcely be prepared for this attitude, and it frequently proves disarming. Reactivating certain ancient wheezes which used to pay off before the sisterhood sharpened up to them, we now offer our current treatment of the following:

The FEEDING THE DOG STALL can still be of use but needs a little refurbishing. Here we suggest indirection. Do not ask her to go with you while you feed Murgatroyd, but begin merely by saying you have forgotten to do it and shrug your shoulders plaintively. Since most women love, or pretend to love, dogs, she will usually volunteer to go with you. This is your cue to thank her effusively as though she were a rare sort. Upon arrival, do not risk giving Murgy the ration of dry dog meal which you usually feed him, but be sure to have on hand some favorite tidbits that will tempt (since you fed him earlier anyway). If he should disdain his snack, the girl may become hostile and who wants that?

The INTERIOR DECORATING PITCH stirs the nesting instincts latent in all women, but, once again, we say make haste slowly. In an apologetic manner state that you would like to show her your apartment, but, unfortunately, this is now out of the question. You are in process of redoing it and everything is a litter of fabric swatches, Italian leather samples, old Fortuny prints, odd lamps, etc. Infer that it is all hopelessly confusing to you, and, impressed by your incompetence, she will probably insist upon going there straightaway. She will herself ask to see your bedroom. Once there, if you can engage her in spirited conversation on quilted bedcovers, one thing may lead to another.

IN THE NEIGHBORHOOD ANYWAY

Sometime, by genuine chance, you may have to pass your digs when you are out with a date. If the neighborhood is nice and the apartment building attractive, you might casually indicate it in passing, but make no allusion to stopping by for a drink. She will wonder what manner of man you are, and a girl whose curiosity is aroused is already half committed. This method requires the utmost forebearance and is not for eager beavers. Don't attempt it if you have had a couple of drinks, or you will find yourself inviting refusal, and she will have gained strength from having bested you.

A BLUEBEARD bachelor with many honorable scars confides that the following has served him well on occasion:

Appear on her doorstep with unshaven phiz (after barber-

Feeding-the-dog stall.

shop hours, of course) as you are about to depart together for dinner. Explain that you didn't want to keep her waiting, besides, shaving twice a day is a bore (hereby implying great masculinity). At this point, not wishing to acknowledge that she, too, owns a razor, she may take you by the ear and lead you to your apartment; hence, precedent is established. Next, please.

REVOLVER GAG

As a pretext for stopping at your apartment, say that you have forgotten your wallet (no argument here) and then tell her to sit in the car because you will be right out. Then, as though it were an afterthought, say that, although the neighborhood looks nice enough, there have been several unmentionable crimes committed recently. Follow this by offering her an oversize derringer which you extract from the glove compartment, spinning the chamber in a businesslike manner as you hand it to her before leaving. Soon you will hear the tapping of her little heels as she rushes to join you for protection.

INSIDE STUFF

The bachelor's apartment should be as much a well-oiled machine as a place to receive mail and store dirty laundry. It should be predominantly masculine, but not to the point of making a girl feel self-conscious or seem out of place. Leering moose heads, varnished muskellunges, and tarnished trophies should be kept to the minimum, so that she doesn't feel that she has violated the smoking room of an athletic club.

If your furniture is of your own choosing, it might as well be modern. Period stuff may recall memories of her parents and home, imposing a morality, through association, foreign to contemporary décor. Blatant overhead lighting is *verboten;* low-keyed table lamps provide soft, flattering illumination and easy access to the switch. Wall-to-wall carpeting eliminates cold floors; a thick pile not only lends a luxuriant air, but invites sprawling. It also improves the acoustics and may break your fall should you run afoul of a judo expert.

A generously proportioned studio couch can be an end in itself or serve admirably as a bull pen for a few warm-up pitches. Placed near the couch, an extra-large coffee table, charged with such items as cigarettes, ash trays, Kleenex, etc., will help maintain progress, saving you the interruption of fetching and carrying while she collects her wits in solitude. Couches, chairs, hassocks should all be low, hinting at the horizontal, but we demur at the isolated comfort of the unassailable contour chair (an outsized chastity belt if we ever saw one).

Feminine appointments and paraphernalia should lurk, conveniently but surreptitiously, in the drawers of the powder room if you have such. A bar is convenient for dispensing a steady flow of liquor. There is less tendency for her to say, "Never mind, it's getting late," if you don't have to knock the neighbors up to borrow ice cubes. A well-stocked bar, which anticipates her taste in drinks rather than have her make do with something she really doesn't care for, can hasten the course of events.

FALSE FRONT

Phineas R., one of those perennially juvenile-looking fellows, had a taste for young fry who have barely reached the legal age of delinquency. He lulled their inhibitions with the unique appearance of his bar. With its peppermint-candy-striped wallpaper and cute wire-backed chairs, painted white with tables to match, the effect was of an innocent, old-fashioned ice-cream parlor. He had even placed containers with straws and paper napkins at each table and had thought to install a magazine rack along one wall. The drinks that he featured were lethal confections, served in flare-topped soda glasses, to be sipped with straws. The result was that these sweet, young things were disarmed by such nostalgic fripperies.

Other impedimenta that do much to make a guest wish to come and linger longer are: a fireplace, a phonograph (see Serenade), a cooling system for hot spells, and a television set with remote control. Television is better used as an inducement to come to the apartment than as a reason to remain. Avoid the longer programs and constantly belittle the entertainment. Subtle dexterity in manipulating the remote control can give the effect of a faulty tube or mechanical failure. Watching fights is good; they are brief and seem to stimulate some girls. A swimming pool and a tennis court would imply an estate rather than an apartment, but you can dream, can't you?

RAIN ON THE ROOF. Alex B., sometimes known as The Scourge of Beverly Hills, has one additional refinement, which he filched from the celebrated Beachcomber Restaurant, and that is an artificial rain system that drips heavily and audibly into the planter that girts his whole house. Many a young chick has put up for the night because he hospitably offered her shelter from the elements.

LATE SNACK

A well-stocked larder frequently pays off. Girls, more than men, get sudden hunger pangs. For the famished doll who becomes ravenous after restaurant hours can easily be in-

duced to enjoy a late snack at your place, especially if you
know her gastronomical weaknesses and idly mention one of
them in appetite-arousing terms. For instance, to say, "Darling, I could go for some scrambled eggs dressed with sour
cream and Beluga caviar. How about you?" might be all that
would be necessary to get some otherwise recalcitrant biddy
on home ground. We offer the above menu because we think
there is something compromisingly like breakfast in sharing
eggs together, yet the added touch of caviar gives a festive
air. But, bear in mind, a kitchen is a bright, wholesome place,
conducive to downright friendliness rather than passion, so
DO NOT EAT THERE. Retire to the dim lights with a bottle of
chilled wine to sustain mood and momentum. Keep such
engrossing snares as chess sets, Scrabble boards, and dart
games out of sight, for time flies by so harmlessly when these
are readily available.

You *bon vivants,* who wish to indulge your fancy a little,
get hold of a silent valet and hang your pants and dinner
jacket on it as well as shirt and black tie. Nothing suggests
the man about town more readily than a minor touch like
this. It makes you apparently in demand and hints at gaiety
in the offing.

The FORBIDDEN ROOM fob-off is a dandy. If your apartment
is commodious, and you are not too concerned about money,
follow the example of Gregory B. and install a completely
equipped boudoir: cosmetics, perfume, comb and brush set,
dressing table, and all. It must be kept immaculate and
appear uninhabited. You will say it is reserved for your
sleepy-time girl, and that its chaste character has never been
violated. This silent challenge may provoke wonder and accomplish what hours of persuasion failed to do. The bed linen
must at all times be fresh and unwrinkled and, for the last

*Gregory B. slowly extracts a key from his pocket
and tentatively opens the door.*

exquisite touch, you could have the pillow and sheets mono-
grammed with question marks on either side of your last
initial. Granted this indicates matrimonial intentions, but a
simple shrug of your shoulders when the girl looks at you
quizzically can hardly be regarded as a firm offer. Yes, keep
the wastebaskets clean; one rouge-smeared piece of Kleenex
and the whole elaborate structure collapses.

To have such a room is one thing, but to present it properly
like the true master, Gregory B., is even more important.
During the "Let me show you the rest of my apartment"
swindle, Gregory gave the tour a haunting Bluebeard appeal
by pausing in front of the door of the room described above,
considering the girl meditatively a moment, then, slowly ex-
tracting a key from his pocket, he tentatively opened the
door with faint trace of reluctance.

A less elaborate but even more rewarding floor plan is
that of George S., the laziest man we know. Thinking only
of his own comfort, he innocently stumbled upon something
good. Being naturally indolent, and antisocial as far as large
gatherings were concerned, he had bunched all comforts,
conveniences, and attractions in his large sleeping quarters.
His unheated living room and dinette area were quite bare
and austere, and what chairs he had were more conducive to
good posture than ease. The only bath had to be reached
through his bedroom so, when a girl went to wash her hands,
she was instantly struck with the contrast. On her return she
invariably would say, "Why don't we sit in there by that nice
fire?" indicating the spider's nest. Sighing and knocking out
his pipe, George would follow her like a patient St. Bernard
and flop on the king-sized bed which, by no accident, faced
a built-in television at its foot. In no time at all, and without
invitation, she would kick off her I. Millers, join him to watch

her favorite program, and there they were and there you are.

CLOTHES AND THE MAN

We see that, up till now, we have said nothing of the bachelor's personal appearance or attire. Since his wardrobe is kept in his apartment, we think this as good a place as any to squeeze in a few remarks about what may be a touchy subject. Most every man is convinced that his taste in clothes (within his budget) is above criticism. This blind belief accounts for the appalling welter of garments, socks, ties, etc., that are offered for sale by unconscionable manufacturers and haberdashers.

No two humans are exactly alike (except Eskimos) and the endless variety of formations and malformations, inherited or acquired, is impressive. There are men who, emerging from the shower to the locker room, look like something polished off by Phidias on a good day; yet, when these Attic gods pile into their clothes, they have a bumpkin look compared to some rachitic, spindly cadaver who towels off, steps into a few yards of gabardine, and suddenly becomes as debonair as Fred Astaire. The natty chap who can wear almost anything is the despair of his confrere who dare not bandage his Adam's apple with a bow tie, who looks like a missionary in a Homburg or Panama, and is obviously miscast in a patterned sport shirt. There is just no use in bucking against it. When a fellow whom Nature has designated as a conservative ventures forth in a tattersall vest, he is as ridiculous and pitiful as a pimply-faced adolescent whose voice splits as he nonchalantly says, "How's tricks, baby?" to some little dream boat.

A good tailor is the silent accomplice of the bachelor, whether he has the teardrop figure of the endomorph or the

V-shaped physique of Cary Grant. Conspire with this man of the needle. His is the art of concealment; he disguises or eliminates all your natural failings: lordosis, knock-knees, unequal legs, uneven shoulders, paunches, and protrusions in general. Don't mar the bumpless silhouette he gives you by bulging the pockets with junk. Carry a thin cigarette case and a flat wallet (no problem) or, still better, that small Diners' Club Book and be a millionaire for a month.

A studied imperfection, in an otherwise faultless ensemble, can sometimes induce the laying on of hands by the kind of girl who can't resist straightening a crooked picture. A tie slightly askew, a handkerchief spilling out, or a single dangling forelock may be all that's necessary for her to make the gesture of affectionate familiarity from which she cannot easily retreat. Many a wise wolf has used this cocker-spaniel approach profitably.

Alors, it is not for you to dazzle but conform. You can let yourself go a little in the sportswear department, but that's about it. Unless you have reason for confidence, don't take her to the beach because you may prove a disappointment to each other and discover a mutual distaste for the task that lies before you.

Heaven forbid that a man of your age get mixed up with some little broad of the blue-jean set, but, if so, use the old psychology, "If you can't beat 'em, join 'em." Put on the leather jacket and T-shirt uniform of this coterie who all dress precisely alike in order to prove their individuality, but with this sneaky difference: bathe regularly, use deodorants, and change the T-shirt frequently. The object of your desire may tire of the animal magnetism of your gamey rivals as she picks up your cologne spoor.

Now we're not going to waste your time or ours with fash-

1   **2**   **3**

MOTIVES FOR MARRIAGE   *(Female)*

GRAPH 2

GRAPH BASED ON TOTAL MARRIAGES 1956 AS REPRESENTING 100%.
(Same as 1955)

GRAPH 1:   *a. Love*
b. Companionship
c. Sexual compatibility
d. Maternal desire
e. Rebellion against parental ties
f. Afraid of dark
g. To pool Raleigh cigarette coupons
with man with similar tastes

GRAPH 3:   *a. Because she was asked*

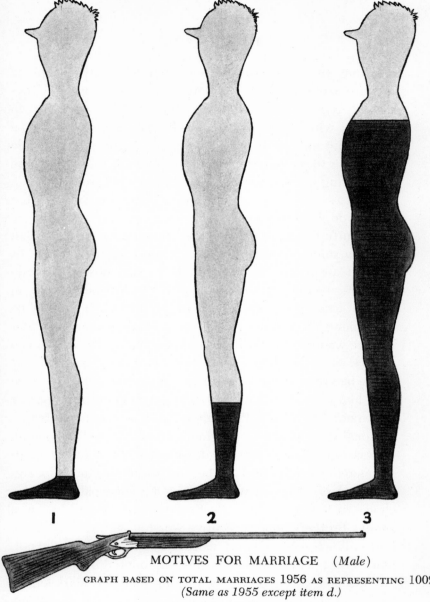

MOTIVES FOR MARRIAGE *(Male)*

GRAPH BASED ON TOTAL MARRIAGES 1956 AS REPRESENTING 100%.
(Same as 1955 except item d.)

GRAPH 2

GRAPH 3: *a. Can't remember*

GRAPH 1: *a. Love*
b. Companionship
c. Sexual compatibility
*d. Desire for male heir in order
   to retain title to principality*
e. Rebellion to parental ties
*f. To pool Raleigh cigarette coupons
   with girl with similar tastes*

ion hints that can easily be culled from a frayed copy of *Esquire* while you wait for a haircut. In general, wear clothes that fit, socks that match, shoes that glisten, and, when in doubt, a white shirt. Your over-all color may be that of a mouse, but at least be sleek. The main purpose of the male costume is to provide a shifting neutral background for those scintillating ingénues from eighteen to eighty, so submit.

The case history we now present points up the fact that clothes do make the man.

Recently Clyde S. called us in desperate straits. He had been pursuing a carhop (of good family) for several months without auspicious success. Lately he had observed something vague and withdrawn about her even when he was in his best form. We hesitated to call this attitude of hers by its right name, i.e., indifference, because Clyde was an old client and we wanted to place him. We knew that loss of confidence was far worse for him than merely being perplexed.

We had reviewed his case in our files before our conference with him in person. We decided to give him our most potent treatment, The C & N Pygmalion No. 1, which amounts to a personal slum-clearance program, physical as well as mental. It was our opinion that Clyde dressed like a rather mild-mannered assassin (perhaps because of his spectacles, octagonal rimless). His hair was overlong, his color pallid, and his choice in ties uproarious. By Friday night we had him in a Brooks Brothers minor-executive worsted with double vents, button-down shirt, red vest, narrow black tie with small knot, black tassel loafers, and all of this surmounted by a crew cut. His spectacles were now wide tortoise shell with dark lenses. His mustache was gone; in fact, everything was altered except his fingerprints. We'd even applied our instant sun-tan oil to give him that Palm Springs look. This outward transformation was carried to the interior by making him commit to memory "Nudnick's Opening."[1] Satisfied that he was letter perfect, we sent him off, chin up.

The next afternoon Clyde came by for our critique. As he came in the door, we could see that he was a changed man.

"Hi, fellas," he said, pouring himself three fingers of our best, without waiting to be asked.

"How did it go?" we asked.

"I drink to your shining, combined genius," he said, raising his glass. "Things couldn't have been better. I actually don't know what happened, but something worked."

Clyde was more than effusive in his gratitude. We were happy for him and told him that we were closing his file with a *cum laude* sticker.

"Great!" he said. "This is really my day. Say, I almost forgot to tell you that I was promoted to general sales manager with a big raise and a fat expense account."

"When did this happen?" we asked.

"Yesterday. It slipped my mind. I was so concerned about Olivia."

"You told her?"

"Now that you mention it, I believe I did. We were driving to her apartment, as I remember."

"Hmmmmm," we both remarked.

UNEQUAL YOKEFELLOWS

A roommate is a rival and a nuisance, a wolf in *your* clothing. The genuine Nimrods of the bachelor set love alone and like it. Only economic necessity can be admitted as sufficient rea-

---

1   We are not at liberty to disclose the nature of "Nudnick's Opening" in print.

son for an otherwise free spirit to submit to the indignity of
of having a yokefellow. Seldom can an equitable arrangement
be worked out for sharing the premises for romantic purposes. If two people live together, one always dominates (or
learns to) through browbeating, bribery, or blackmail. When
we think of the long dreary nights spent in late shows,
deserted bars, all-night drugstores, or in just plain trudging
up and down, waiting for an all clear, while some usurper we
could mention by name is highhandedly pretending that
what is ours is his, we could—well—never mind.

Even if you should be on the inside looking out, the situation still wants perfection. For instance, if your latest little
acquisition knows you share your apartment, she will tighten
up her feathers, expecting, momentarily, in spite of your
assurances to the contrary, the boisterous intrusion of your
brassy, leering bunkie. The best way to allay her doubts in
this regard is to begin the rendezvous by establishing his
absence, apologetically but firmly. Some bald-faced lie, to
the effect that you regret that she won't be able to meet the
dear fellow because he's off for the weekend, should suffice;
but don't forget to put the chain lock on the door. As a hedge
against his untimely return, you can show her a sealed collect
telegram, previously hidden near the door, which will explain
his sudden pounding at your palings and account for your
mumbled words as you pass currency out into the darkness
to stall him off. If he's not too drunk, she may think nothing amiss.

Signal systems have some merit if they are adopted in good
faith. The dubious raising and lowering of blinds or switch-
ing on and off of lights gives a cloak-and-dagger air which is
titillating only to iron-nerved Mata Haris. The best reply to
this knotty problem we can recall is that practiced by two

former seamen who had learned to honor signals through years of training. When the apartment was in use, the incumbent ran up the pennant which indicated "Owner aboard" while his shipmate stood the watch.

When a liaison is well established, the very presence of your roommate may concern her no longer; she may even propel him to the door, clapping his beret on his head and thrusting him out into the rain as the spirit moves her. On the other hand, as her natural proprietary feelings mount, she may, one enchanted evening, do the same to you, and then, die-hard, you will realize that sharecropping is for the boids.

7. Serenade

Gone is the ukulele, and with it the advantage of the slightly talented over the tone deaf. The phonograph is a great equalizer and has made music a commodity rather than an art, so that today the light-footed layman, clutching an album of records, stands on equal terms with his more gifted bachelor brother. This situation is in line with the modern tendency for all recreation to become spectator sports, save one.

Phonograph records can supplant candy and flowers and are as disarming as drink. If she has no record player, there is no reason to feel frustrated; simply take her by her hot little hand and lead her to your apartment. The idea is to get from Orpheus to Morpheus with as much dispatch as politeness will allow.

A phonograph is an indispensable item in the properly furnished bachelor home. The random mixture of ballad and bop that emanates from the radio is unreliable and frequently disconcerting for the business at hand. First of all, get a good record changer. The gravel-like sound of a tone arm that has bounced out of the groove and is playing a felt serenade has often proven a fatal interruption to a bachelor's progress. Some moments are never to be retrieved. The advent of the long-playing record proves a real boon here, reducing the chances of this sort of thing occurring to one in five over the conventional waxes.

Mood music is an almost necessary adjunct to romance. There is, however, the constant danger of becoming engrossed in the music itself. Beware of listening wholeheartedly; rather keep up a patter germane to your real purpose. Should she happen to be a jive hound, you may find the old Capehart no friend but a rival. So before her next visit abolish her favorites and get into the music-for-dreaming department.

Dancing with the target for the night, in the privacy of your own apartment, may serve as an excuse to hold her close, but you can lose her this way as well, especially if you are a *good* dancer. Dancing, according to Havelock Ellis, is a substitute for you-know-what, and who wants oleo when he can have butter? Some girls truly love to dance, so, if her pleasure seems too complete here, pull up lame and get back to that couch.

DISC JOCKEY

We should like to brighten up proceedings by introducing one. Peter P. Pete is a specialist in high fidelity (you should forgive the expression) to accomplish low purposes and has developed this particular operation to trap-door perfection. The following sets forth his general M.O.

Peter soon fixes on the girl's natural taste in music and wastes no time in attempting to convert her to his own, for if it's Montavani or Kostelanetz she wants, instead of Palestrina, then so be it. Feeding her the above confections like a kidnaper, his next move is the "Our Song" wheeze. He is of the opinion that here it is best to let her appear to choose

"Gone is the ukulele and with it the advantage of the slightly talented over the tone-deaf."

it in the way that she would select a card, just any card, from a prestidigitator. The song being chosen, Pete feels that he now has a climax to build toward in his evening of music. Almost invariably the song will be of the ballad variety, although we know a cozy pair of sport fans that swoon every time they hear the "How Are You Fixed for Blades?" commercial.

But to return to Peter. Acknowledging the convenience of the long-playing records, he, nevertheless, is proudest of having made the team, so to speak, on numerous occasions by means of a carefully selected stack of standard 78s. His pride is comparable to the huntsman who gets his deer with a bow and arrow. Of course, needless to say, he had checked his automatic changer with the casual ease of a Dutchman about to split the Kohinoor diamond. To accomplish his ends with one well-chosen pile is to bring off quite a parlay. But Pete has admitted coming a cropper, recalling wryly the time that "Lead, Kindly Light" showed up on the flip side of "Love For Sale," the girl in this case being a good Presbyterian.

Pete roughly classifies music into two categories: No. 1— Prelude, and No. 2—Pay-off Stuff. The character of the former is generally romantic and that of the latter, rhythmic. (It is here that our write-in service may prove invaluable.)

Pete is a bit of a philosopher, as well as a disc jockey, and we'd like to give you a slice of his thinking. Since the first woman presented a gadget-happy male (whose best effort to date was a crude flint arrowhead) with a bouncing baby boy and said, "Now, let's see you top that!" she has regarded herself as the undefeated champion inventor of all time and hasn't been seriously impressed with his tinkering from that day forward. This attitude, says Pete, applies to anything with wheels or wires, so don't expect her to show the slightest genuine interest in the workings of your hi-fi system. If you wish to spend a truly coaxial evening with her, lay off the input talk and the chatter about tweeters and sound reflexes, but just plop on her favorite tune, turn the volume down, and treat your whole damn operation as if it were a 1932 Orthophonic. It may seem like going to buy groceries with a 4.5 Ferrari, but who cares? First things first.

MODUS OPERANDI

Some of the most appealing melodies ever written are to be found in the repertory of opera. The playing of a complete version of an opera is inadvisable, however, because, interspersed between the melodic portions, are the recitatives. These are long passes of conversation, half sung, half spoken, for the purpose of furthering the plot and keeping tab on the number of corpses, opera being a notoriously internecine affair with a mortality rate greater than a Fourth-of-July weekend. The sudden intrusion of voices, so vivid in modern reproduction, can be quite startling at the wrong moment, especially if it happens to be an irate basso demanding vengenance. Listen, if you must, to the exquisite caterwauling as expressed from the compressed *embonpoint* of assorted sopranos, tenors, etc., but, for landsakes, don't let her read the libretto! One after another, these librettos are nothing but the stories of betrayed womanhood (*Faust, Don Juan,* etc.), so, for your pains, you may fetch up with a fat lip as she squares things for Madame Butterfly after all these many years.

8. The Line

It can hardly be expected in a book such as this, which may fall into alien hands, that we reveal any of the standard male approaches, some of which, though slightly hoary, are still paying off nightly. But, without breach of confidence, we feel that the topic should be discussed generally. We counsel observation of one basic tenet—never change a winning pitcher or, in other words, if you are doing well with your own personal approach, don't seek to alter or embroider on same if the results satisfy.

GENERALITIES

Some general concepts should be noted. These are:

1. Tailor the line to the girl. Never try to bring down a tigress with bird shot and never shoot a dove with an express rifle.
2. Pace yourself. In other words, stop to observe the effect of your pitch and don't fall in love with the sound of your own voice.
3. Have at least one alternate approach. Girls sometimes compare notes, and if you happen to date a girl friend of a girl friend, they can crucify you in

your absence. It is a myth that girls don't talk about their affairs—not that they frequently admit surrender in so many words to another chum, but THEY DO TALK!

4. Never introduce subjects which may be of interest in themselves unless you are merely passing time in a public place. Fine conversation may be indulged in after the fact, if you are so minded. Only a fool would introduce a controversial subject when alone with a lovely pigeon. Religion and politics are to be avoided like mumps. Around election time Democrats are loathe to go bed with Republicans (and vice versa), except for purposes of conversion. Decide for yourself whether you want an adversary or an accomplice.

5. Do not appear to possess in too great a degree any of the following virtues:

   a. Affluence
   b. Reliability
   c. Sentimentality
   d. Thoughtfulness
   e. Ambition
   f. Love for children
   g. Or being too damn handy around the house.

The reason why a revelation of the above traits can operate against you is because these are what a girl seeks in a husband, and, taking a long view of you, she may deny you your immediate reward and sell you out for the prospect of a handful of thrown rice.

FLATTERY

Flattery is the art of telling welcome lies, but such lies must

"Only a fool would introduce a controversial subject when alone with a lovely person."

contain just enough truth to make them credible. A certain sprightliness and gaiety should be infused into the moment of delivery. If there is a halting or reluctant air about its presentation, a lie or compliment is robbed of its potency. Don't lose out for want of that last little dash of enthusiasm, the big pink bow that makes a Christmas gift of an article of merchandise.

Flattery is an inexpensive commodity; the cost of materials is reasonable since words are cheap and the labor is your own. Next to charm and money, the ability to flatter is one of the most appealing traits that women appreciate in a man. It is unlike the other two noble attributes in that it is most effective when undetected. If it is noticed favorably, it is confused with natural charm, and often serves just as well.

The astute flatterer must, first of all, be observant; a woman likes to feel that she is noticed. Approving references to her hair, her perfume, her clothes, etc., never fail to please but are doubly pleasing when ornamented with particulars. Generalities are for the inept, or husbands. For instance, if she is wearing an attractive gown, the advanced flatterer will venture that it is by Dior or Balenciaga. Should his guess prove correct, she is pleased and impressed, and, if not correct, she is successfully flattered. So, either way, he wins.

PLAYING FOOTSIE   The compleat specialist in the art of conning a girl is, to our way of thinking, Bernie B. His particular flim-flam, if used for openers, requires the setting of a beach or swimming pool. He begins literally at her feet, remarking of their beauty immediately. Since almost no one has pretty feet anyway, she will be surprised but will sit still for it. Then Bernie strengthens the deception by being specific. If, as sometimes happens, her second toe extends further than her big toe (known as the great toe in

England), he launches into a cadenza which he calls Praise of the Second Phalange, scuttling back to the ancient Greeks for sculptural examples that alone rival the beauty of her tootsies. This unique bamboozle works equally well with the compliment-hardened belle or just Plain Jane. Best of all, it helps to get her shoes and stockings off on future dates, since any woman likes to put her best foot forward.

Every change of a woman's hairdo is of earth-shaking importance to her. If you make a point of remarking that she had it cut shorter than formerly, or has changed her part from one side to the other, she will be delighted that you remembered. It is not always necessary that you approve of these little changes. In fact, sometimes disapproval gently expressed with thoughtful, constructive criticism can convey a greater concern on your part than casual praise; besides, it takes longer, and she enjoys being the center of attention.

COLOR FILTER

Upon meeting for the first time, a girl whose hair is currently blonde, you can indulge in a two-edged compliment by saying that ordinarily you don't like blondes but that, somehow, she is an exception. This approval of her present shade pleases her, but she also feels a security within herself that you would like her hair in its natural state; that you are not a victim of mere artifice, but would like her as she really is. (This is especially reassuring to blonde Chinese girls.)

It is possible, while all the previous prattle was going on, she may have been scrutinizing your own raven temples and wondering just how to tell you that, after all, gray hair is truly becoming and lends distinction to a man's appearance. If she patronizingly adds that you are only as old as you feel you are, then scratch her off your list. Anyway, she probably has a late date with some young whippersnapper still in his forties.

ON THE SCENT

The sharp bachelor must have a nose for, as well as an eye for, details. He should learn to identify and remember various popular perfumes. When he compliments a woman on her choice of scent, she will no doubt wear it again; then he should be sure to comment about it, recognizing that she has done it to please him, and so establish himself as an appreciative escort.

C & N DELAYED-REACTION COMPLIMENT

Most women enjoy being praised for what they are but they enjoy, even more, being praised for what they are *not*. A woman's credulity is as elastic as a pelican's bill, so don't hesitate at the preposterous; it will be well received. Extol some quality she does *not* possess. Sometimes this offbeat homage, totally undeserved at first, may become her just due because she will try to be what you say she is. In this way it is possible to bring about a desired change in an otherwise attractive girl. For instance, the creature in question, though charming in many respects, might be shy and conservative, with a consequently high melting point; to alter this you should try the C & N Delayed-Reaction Compliment by telling her that you feel, contrary to outward indications, she is truly a little devil, a real fireball at heart. Reiterate this thought frequently in different ways. We know a little bluestocking who, in a few short weeks, became a virtual harridan, living for pleasure alone, after repeated doses of the above formula.

I JUST LOVE YOU

In our college days at Old Piltdown U., when we were more or less amateur consultants for other fraternity members, we discovered the value of the simple, direct approach as well as its attendant risks. At that time the vogue in the treatment of coeds was studied nonchalance, the assuming of a sophisticated mien approaching insouciance. Although little was actually admitted in bull sessions, C & N, reading between the lines, came to the conclusion that few among us were getting the bag limit. However, there appeared to be one notable exception, Kirby L., who returned late, night after night, seemingly limp with success. Pressing the matter closely, we cross-questioned him and he finally told us that, contrary to current practice, he simply told all the girls he met that he just loved them. This naïve system had the virtue of novelty at this particular time and apparently brought astonishing results. Deciding not to accept this method without further laboratory proof, we recommended its use to one Everett C., a brother who had been notable for a staggering series of failures in the dame department. He submitted to our advice and, two weeks later, he was married on his graduation day. We hear from him each Christmas, and the card he sends has a picture of himself and his annually increasing family. We think we detect a mean look between the eyes that could be meant for us. So much for the perils and virtues of simplicity.

The CAVALIER APPROACH is frequently successful because women still enjoy being treated as ladies, although they secretly feel that man is a damn fool for doing it. A woman is most desirous of being treated like a lady just after she has proven she is not. The old gag of treating charwomen like duchesses, and duchesses like charwomen, may be fine

"We think we detect a mean look between the eyes that could be meant for us."

for the boulevard, but not for the boudoir. Sometimes it is fun to treat a bum like a princess, but if she embraces the part too enthusiastically, you can waste a whole evening before she comes to your senses. She may be impressed, grow sentimental, and try to remember how she used to say no.

We suppose it is possible for a bachelor to appear to be a gentleman although it may incommode him at times. He would do well to conceal this better part of his nature or he will find that women will impose upon it. This better self should be liberally overlaid with an air of rascality, because a cloak of naughtiness serves to make important things seem inconsequential to both parties involved.

Jerome K., a celibataire well known to us, has had results with the dodge of kissing a girl immediately upon his arrival for his first date. She is too surprised to resist. It seems all in good fun, but the preliminaries are now over. The ice is broken and there remains but one point of contention. It is no longer a question of kissing him good night, and hoping to satisfy him with that, but the battle is already joined. She has lost an outpost and must fall back to the defense of the citadel itself.

The perplexing case of Henry H. defies pigeonholing, but deserves inclusion, so we'll pop it in right about here. Henry best illustrates how apparently disarming merely being polite and pleasant can be. We have observed him fraternizing and we know that he puts nothing in their drinks, employs no form of mesmerization, mutters no threats or bribes, and yet, time and again, right from under our noses, he has gone off into the night with the prize dish of the evening—and almost as if she had asked *him*. We at one time considered the hypothesis that Henry might actually *like* women as folks and had some way of communicating this fact to them as some people seem to be able to talk to birds, but we soon dismissed this notion as preposterous. . . . And yet? . . .

"OMNE ANIMALE EST TRISTE"

If any one thing separates the men from the boys among bachelors it is their conduct immediately following success. There is no denying the letdown; the world's illusion has vanished and it is Monday morning in your soul and bones. A cigarette, or a sandwich, has more appeal than Helen of Troy, but the wise man does not betray his real feelings. What may seem to be truth and reality is the greatest delusion of all. JUST WAIT! Valiantly bridge these few minutes with a display of affection; things are never as bad as they seem. You will observe that, contrary to your own inclinations, the young lady will be genuinely affectionate, in fact, never more so. At this particular moment she needs reassurance because she now feels that she may have lost her charm, or perhaps mislaid it. To allay such misgivings, the shrewd and gallant thing to do is to telephone her the next day so that she can thank you for the flowers that you dispatched to her earlier that morning. Flowers and candy, prosaic to be sure, like the daily newspaper, are noticed more in their absence. But now, since you are panting to get on with this book, turn to the ensuing chapter where you might learn something to your advantage about gifts in general.

9. Gifts

Better than the gift of gab is a gift itself. A gift might be defined as a three-dimensional flattery, and there is not a woman who breathes whose pulse doesn't quicken at the sight of a beribboned package, the smaller the better. A show of gratitude in a woman is usually spontaneous, sincere, and short-lived, and can be mistaken for passion. In the matter of gifts, the bachelor has a position of clear advantage. His offerings have the thrilling, compromising aspects of bribes, while the husband's tardy presents are deserved rewards long overdue.

Men are sentimental about women; women are sentimental about themselves. Their birthdays and anniversaries are affairs of great moment to them and become so, consequently, to men, especially if they should forget them. Men are phlegmatic about their own natal days, etc. Ask any retail merchant, florist, or jeweler how much business he did on Father's Day ... but nothing! Now Mother's Day (Philip Wylie notwithstanding) ... there's a real bonanza. "And *why* not?" the distaff side will ask in unison with an inevitable reference to something about "the best years of their lives." (Indignation is woman's greatest forensic weapon, and for centuries it has carried the day for her in every encounter.) Let it be understood that we are not pro-testing, complaining, or proposing to change things as they are, but merely bringing certain facts to your attention, so that you may employ this knowledge to your interest. In other words, women demand (with a sigh or a longing look, to be sure) largesse, or tribute, as their natural heritage, and you, Santa Claus, might just as well go along with the gag.

The LAVISH BARGAIN is a basic principle to hold in mind and that is: ALWAYS GIVE THE BEST. This may sound expen-sive but it ain't necessarily so. For instance, a ten-dollar handkerchief is infinitely better than a ten-dollar blouse... the one is lavish and the other niggardly. Choose your cate-gories wisely and be a winner.

Baubles and bangles, jewelry, that is, must be rated high on the agenda. It has some negotiable value and is enduring. The act of wearing it serves to remind her of the giver con-stantly. If you lack the loot to deluge her with diamonds, investigate the costume jewelry of one of the first houses. Labels are of supreme importance. A lesser gift from an elite establishment often carries more prestige than a better article from the wrong side of the tracks.

If the gift has a personal touch, some reference to herself, like her zodiacal sign, it will convince her that you have given the matter some consideration. Use her birthstone if it is of a semiprecious nature; your thoughtfulness will modify her pique at your economy. Tender and inventive inscrip-tions are always in order, and each trinket should contain just enough gold so that gangrene does not set in.

The HEIRLOOM GAG, though slightly mildewed, works on the sentimental doll. A quaint cameo (obtainable in any antique shop) can be invested with some romantic family balderdash and presented ceremoniously. While not as in-

A woman is never more sincere than when she tells a millionaire she loves him.

criminating as an engagement ring, it obliquely hints of the future, family and fireside, and may dispel her native caution.

MILLIONAIRE'S DILEMMA

Shopping a girl into submission, we admit, perilously resembles true courtship and is an indulgence reserved for the affluent among us. Perhaps now is as good a time as any to consider the plight of the wealthy playboy. Some of these poor chaps suffer from a peculiar but understandable form of self-doubt. For instance, if a girl should tell one of the above types that she loves him, he is just neurotic enough to question it. Sheer nonsense! A woman is never more sincere than when she tells a millionaire she loves him. Most women are extremely sentimental about money, but we are quick to note exceptions. Some are *not* interested in a man for his money. These heiresses would just as soon have a man without a sou to his noble family name.

THE FLABBERGASTER

A bachelor baron of Bel Air, jaded by success, in an inspired moment came up with this gift twist . . . something under *her* pillow! . . . and this on the first night out! Presumptuous, to be sure, but also provocative and titillating. The "take it for granted" air, he found, made protest seem belated and naïve. His consummate gall either fascinated or intimidated his victims. The most unsettling feature of this act was its very preposterousness; it brought about acquiescence through hilarity, if we can believe him.

10. C & N Grab Bag

TATTOOING Acknowledging the primitive instinct to mutilate oneself in a decorative manner to impress others, we have devised our own tattoos which remove the pain and the consequence of these strange whims. The C & N tattoo is unique in that it is no tattoo at all but looks like the real thing. Actually they are cleverly designed decalcomanias in assorted designs cleverly devised by a Japanese houseboy formerly in our employ. Their prime virtue is that they will not come off but will endure until you use our special solvent, Smirnoff 4711.

The choice of designs should vary with your situation. For instance, to excite tenderness in a girl's bosom, perhaps the conventional "Mother," surmounting your social-security number, would suggest that you are a good home boy as well as employed without your doing anything overt to establish this estimate in the young lady's mind.

If for some reason you wish to kindle jealousy in her bosom, another girl's name might do the trick and at the same time lend a certain glamour beyond your means. Such names as "Ava," "Lana," "Grace," etc., might awaken her to some unsuspected, hidden merit not previously apparent.

Restraint should be the watchword in the employment of

the tattoo ruse. It is a rather precious approach and should not be used if all is well, but only if you are at a complete loss for some angle to jostle her to wakefulness. The whole shooting match could boomerang badly if you have appraised the girl wrongly.

Perhaps we should explain right here that the real inspiration for our temporary tattoo came from learning of the sad plight of Moe D. We happened upon Moe one rainy afternoon at the club, just as he emerged from the shower room. Seeing us, he hastily drew his towel across his chest in what could be construed as a modest gesture. Our curiosity was so piqued by his furtive behavior that we found ourselves inviting him to have a drink with us.

As the afternoon dribbled on, Moe's tongue loosened and he confided to us that, a year or so ago, he had endured the pain of being tattooed and all because of a woman. Since she had accused him of being fickle, in a fit of undying devotion he had had her name etched in clear Bodoni letters across his façade. The irony of fate decreed that she would choose that very evening at Ciro's to inform him that she no longer cared to see him. When Moe began frantically clawing at his shirt front to reveal to her the extent of his affection, she went screaming from the dance floor while a trombone player and three waiters subdued him, prior to flinging him halfway to Mocambo, where he spent the rest of the night mumbling over some Sazeracs.

When we reminded Moe that the world is filled with women and that he might find another with the same name, he looked at us scornfully and silently removed the towel. We read:

GISEELE WORBEJEC PIFFLE

We confessed that this narrowed the field somewhat, and he said that you're damn well right it did. When we ventured that perhaps a reconciliation was in order, Moe only shook his head. It seems that Miss Piffle had decided to change her name and did not wish to be reminded of her former one in any way. She is now pursuing a film career as one Scarlet Slovak and having quite a go at it, as you darn well know.

ASTROLOGY

Astrologers seem to know more than astronomers. An astrologer only needs to know what day it is and own an old almanac to come up with the most amazing things—prophecies, warnings, and the like. By comparison, astronomers are an uninformed lot, always running to the nearest telescope to look at the same old stars.

One of the most remarkable things that a good astrologer can do is to write a blanket forecast for every man, woman, and child born during a certain period of thirty days of any year. Presuming on this latitude of practice, in an otherwise exact science, we have prepared our own C & N horoscopes. We offer two kinds: first, an all-round buckshot type, related to romantic activity in general, and, second, a custom number, designed for your particular girl, with her birth date, day, month, year, and hour all calibrated to a fine point. This latter celestial chart will show that not only are the stars and planets propitious for *l'amour*, but that her actions are preordained, and she would be offending the heavens and old Evangeline Adams herself if she were to continue to hold out another day.

CRYSTAL BALL

If your cupcake is reasonably superstitious, the fortuneteller

". . . you will perhaps find the swami congenial, for, shall we say, $5.00?"

twist may be helpful. The main idea is to get to him first. While not actually dishonest, you will perhaps find the swami congenial for, shall we say, $5.00. Apart from enumerating your fine qualities, if he suggests that you are about to inherit a considerable sum of money, this will have a heartening effect on the lady. But for the clincher, if you wish to go so far, the seer could also predict an early demise for you. Most women fancy themselves in black, Continental and all.

HANDWRITING

For any of you dear readers who think that handwriting analysis is a phony bit, take heed and listen. It is truly frightening what one of these experts, even those found in bars and restaurants, can tell from a few written words. So unless your character is sans reproach, don't submit in the company of any girl you have hopes about, or at least don't use your own handwriting. A few hours diligently spent can give anyone reasonably adroit with a pencil a fair facsimile of the hand of some great genius, examples of which, living or dead, are easily found in the public library. Don't, however, choose loosely any name that just happens to be well known to you. The following brief story should be sufficient warning.

Homer Q. came to us for a bit of coaching before his first date with a stock girl at Warner Bros. toward whom he had nothing but the warmest of feelings and the blackest of intentions. This girl didn't like playboys but admired men who could do creative things. She was especially fond of music. Homer informed us that he, too, had an insatiable appetite for all things cultural. Taking our cue from this, we suggested that Homer take her to the Stunned Ox where they had duo pianists and a handwriting expert to take care of any lulls in the conversation. We thought it a brilliant stroke when we hit upon the idea that, for the two days prior to the evening in question, Homer should bone up on the handwriting of some great musician.

That Homer chose Richard Wagner for his chicanery was his own doing and not our responsibility. When he came complaining to us that Wagner, in his private life, was an unscrupulous, foul, two-timing scoundrel, we tried to console him by saying we thought it remarkable that he should happen upon someone so like himself, sharing all his personal traits and having talent besides. Homer seemed to take umbrage at this and departed shortly thereafter. Later we sat down to a choice Châteaubriand for two, each holding a cold portion to his cheek while quietly regarding the other with his good eye and pondering the folly of philanthropy.

HYPNOTISM

The recent wide interest aroused in the public mind by experiments in hypnotism makes it necessary for us to state our position in this regard. There is something clinical about the use of hypnotism that is repugnant to us. If a girl doesn't like you without taking an anesthetic, we say the hell with it. We abandoned the use of hypnotism as something sneaky and underhanded after barely five years of experimentation. We found, with few exceptions, that those women who would submit to it willingly were suggestible enough on a conscious level to make its use unnecessary, and the rest couldn't be hypnotized anyway.

A case in point is the sad and ludicrous story of Heathcliff B. Heathcliff was the owner of a number of fine income apartments on Beverly Glen which he had built after futilely trying to acquire ownership of the Girls' Studio Club in Hollywood. His tenants were carefully screened, all female,

"We abandoned the use of hypnotism as something sneaky and underhanded."

under twenty-five, and most of them only seasonably employed, which made rent day a thing for speculation. By
some oversight there was one independent young lady of
means who would have been a beauty without her glasses.
She easily resisted Heathcliff's blandishments, so that he, at
last, resorted to hypnotism, contrary to our warnings. She
was the intellectual type and submitted with alacrity while
he twirled a Phi Beta key (reproduction). While she was
under the spell, he made the posthypnotic suggestion that,
upon awakening, she would think she was Diamond Lil.
When roused, she blinked a couple of times and then, looking at her fingernails, said out of the side of her mouth,
"Hello, handsome. Where'd you get those cute narrow shoulders?" As Heathcliff was about to reply, the kitchen door
opened and Mike, the janitor, came in to fix the faucet. Spy-
ing him, she purred, strutted over, and said: "Kiss me, big
boy." Mike obliged at some length, and then she suggested
that they leave Junior and go upstairs.

Two days later Heathcliff heard they were in Acapulco,
cooing and billing, and she was footing the bills. He was
disconsolate when he came to see us—bemoaning his loss.

"Really, Heathcliff, old boy, why be greedy? You still have
a houseful of talent at that resort of yours."

"But you don't understand," he said. "Janitors like Mike
are hard to find."

C & N EARPHONY

This inexpensive device lends a man the appeal of the bird
with the broken wing and, like a black patch over one's eye,
has, for some obscure reason, a glamorous effect. It seems to
excite pity in the female breast and may start the chain reac-

tion of pity to tenderness to passion (a process that is a reversal of the usual order of romantic events).

The C & N earphony is a lightweight, black plastic article resembling the genuine thing, but without the complexities of batteries, grids, filaments, etc.—being what the name implies, a dummy piece. We originally intended it for our bachelor clientele, but now our greatest demand comes from the married men. Yielding to their clamor, we have produced a modification of the original. The married man's model *insures* deafness in one ear, since it is nothing more or less than an earplug.

The more artful of our earphony users will pretend to complain of its inefficiency while enjoying its virtues. Its greatest appeal for the bachelor is that he can hear what he chooses. For instance, when leaving her apartment on a date, he can cheerfully ask, "Where to?" and then take her to a cheaper spot than the one she named, since she might hesitate to remind him of his sad affliction. Even better, later that night, he can feign not to hear her urgently whispered "No! No!" and smilingly prevail while she says to herself in resignation, "Oh, what the hell!"

DREAM MAN

Some people still go to the theater. It is a pleasant, ice-breaking maneuver for a first date. Television may surpass the legitimate theater and films in the matter of convenience and economy, but not socially. The average girl has access to her own TV set and probably has conjunctivitis from staring at it, night after night, waiting for the phone to ring. The term "to go out with a man" means what it says; hence the theater still has its place. Unless you live in New York, and can afford $6.60 and up per copy, you might as well take her to a movie house or one of those open-air brothels called drive-ins.

The dark privacy of the theater can be wasted if, by chance, you take her to see her "dream man." If she goes on about Marlon Brando too much, begin to drool over the leading lady of the piece. This should shut her up. If she persists, let her open the car door for herself and see how she likes it.

And now, since you have painstakingly committed to memory or sedulously employed much of the foregoing advice, gimmicks, dodges, etc., this inevitably brings you to your probable reward which is

11. A Woman's No

Most women are apt to say "No" to advances at the onset, but there are usually implicit overtones of "Maybe" to the well-tuned male ear. Any man who takes a girl at her word is foolish, and even the girl herself will regard him as a disappointing antagonist. All girls will haggle like secondhand car dealers and expect a run for their money. The seasoned male campaigner will merely affect not to hear until things take a turn for the better and then close the deal quickly.

Naturally an attitude of refusal can only make an object more desirable and, in this way, she contributes to your fuller pleasure ultimately. Complete and ready acquiescence would make most huntsmen feel nonplused for a quick moment and bring about a feeling of having been cheated of the sport of the game.

Talk if you must, but remember, it is easier for a woman to consent actually than verbally. Consent through conversation alone is humiliating as well as bloody unlikely. The game-wise bachelor rarely tries for an explicit "Yes" but plays for the incriminating but thrilling "Oh, but we shouldn't." Observe the "we" (you have been included) and the

In that magpies' nest which is a woman's purse lies a veritable arsenal of defense weapons.

"shouldn't," implying "we are about to." Equally encouraging is a series of muffled noes; generally the word "no" is meaningless and is used merely to set the tempo of progress, like the measured cadence of a coxswain.

Compared with the great variety of approaches and lines, there are very few ways for a woman to say NO; even she may become embarrassed with the monotony of her dialogue. It is advisable to remind her of her lack of invention at every opportunity. In contrast with your own wealth of imagery, fervor, and enthusiasm, her flat negative can give her little pleasure. In seeking to qualify or soften it, she may compromise herself ever so slightly. This is the cue to hammer a wedge into the gap and make her fall back to previously prepared positions, another way of saying that she is fighting a nice losing battle.

In the seclusion of your apartment when things are moving forward and your overtures are well received, it is important to circumvent interruption. A vital trifle to keep in mind is the disposition of her handbag. IT SHOULD ALWAYS BE KEPT WELL OUT OF HER REACH. In that magpie's nest, which is a woman's purse, lies a veritable arsenal of defense weapons: comb, powder, lipstick, nail file, cigarette holder, etc.—so immobilize her and do not permit her to fence and parry with any of the above articles of war. Psychologists say that an attitude or gesture can beget a frame of mind. A woman never seems so unassailable as when she is combing her hair or putting on lipstick. The tempo of things is broken by such feminine gestures; therefore, don't let her terminate happy hostilities with such ease. Muss her up a little, get her shoes off, because there is something erotic in a mild disarray of her person which even she will sense. If a small repair job seems futile, she may relax and accept the situation.

PRECIPITATION NORMAL

To a husband, tears are a means of ordinary communication, but, in the presence of a bachelor, teardrops are infrequent and usually the indication of some temporary emotional upset.

Girls can cry at the drop of the hat. It is a favorite form of self-expression; they actually enjoy it. To "have a good cry" is strictly a feminine notion. There is no doubt that crying or, worse, sobbing can hold up or cancel the game on wet grounds. Joy and tears may be compatible; pleasure and tears are not. Only a cad (and 50 per cent of us are not) would refuse to accept the above truth philosophically. Here, we say, you might as well be gallant, and, as sometimes happens, she may call the next day to apologize and hint at another chance.

Mascara is a hindrance to weeping, for not only does it make a pretty girl look like a raccoon, but it has a tendency to smart and burn. Few women whose eyes are laden with the stuff will frivolously resort to tears. It is wise to encourage the use of mascara through the simple act of flattery.

GIRLS CRY—MEN TALK

What the catcher really says to the pitcher when he walks out to the mound or what actually goes on in a Notre Dame huddle have long been subjects for speculation, but no more so than men talk is to the inquisitive female. Most any girl would love to be a mouse in a men's locker room for an hour or so, whereas no self-respecting male would give a Christmas necktie to overhear the chatter that goes on in the powder room. This is probably because the girls have nothing to say of a personally revealing nature. The reason for this difference is that confession is painful, while bragging

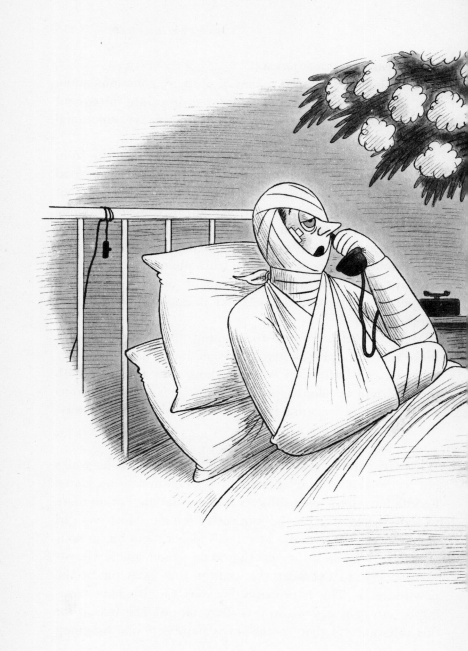

*". . . call us . . . and we will point out just where you
made your mistake."*

is fun. What is a conversation piece for the man is a source of nail biting for the woman. There is, consequently, little Monday-morning quarterbacking among the girls; the pleasures of open retrospection are taboo. In speaking of the same thing the boys enjoy themselves and the girls squirm.

Men talk is kind of a clearinghouse for the boys. Whereas it is not considered cricket to kiss and tell, nevertheless, silence itself is incriminating and an admission of failure is humiliating. In large groups it is regarded as bad taste to be blunt, hence innuendo is the order of the day; but if an eyebrow is lifted out of context, a girl's reputation may become wobbly.

First off, let us remind you that a good listener never interrupts. This applies pertinently and peculiarly to men talk. To get to the point: You are at your club, enjoying a drink after putting in a hard day on the back nine. Some tiger-muscled blowhard comes plopping in from the showerroom, downs your drink, by mistake, of course, and, as he dries himself scrupulously, somehow gets on the subject of his gal's charm and talent in the boudoir, sparing no details. If you are able to forget that you know her as well as he does, and merely listen with a kind of noncommittal interest, all is well. But, by chance, should you get carried away by his enthusiasm and unwittingly say something like, "Boy, she sure is!" then please call us when you are able to get about again, and we will point out just where you made your mistake.

12. Off The Hook

There are certain danger signs which the knowing bachelor perceives but quickly. Like a good boxer who watches the other guy's hands rather than his eyes, our man knows that it is not what the young lady says but what she does that counts. Circumstantial evidence is far more weighty than the direct testimony of her lips; she may not only deceive you but herself. In order to distinguish between mere fervor and sincerity, it is necessary to keep a wary eye on what may seem, at first glance, to be trifling details. We shall try to be more specific: If a girl tells you she loves you, in the straightforward manner of an accomplished liar, this need not deeply concern you. But if she reveals her affection *casually* in little ways, then there may be a cause for alarm. For instance, if she unconsciously clutches your arm and stays close in the presence of other attractive men, she may be genuinely afflicted, so be careful—it can be contagious. Further signs, such as stroking your hair (in public), fussing with your tie or handkerchief, wanting to shop for you, and barraging you with cute, unnecessary phone calls . . . all these are grave indications that things are not as they should be. The time to make your move is at hand. When she says

"If the statement is accompanied by a pair of sox which she knit herself, then drop her while she purls two."

that you are the most incredibly wonderful man she has ever known, don't let this worry you. She may just respect you, and this has little to do with female love. But if the statement is accompanied by a pair of sox which she knit herself, then drop her while she purls two.

There comes a moment in an affair when one party or the other wants out (and it could happen to you). This has little application to one-night stands but only to affairs of some duration where face saving is involved. It is peculiarly a man's problem. When a girl decides she has had it, she is traditionally permitted to be forthright and brutal and need only say, "Good-by," "Au Revoir," "Adios," "Get Lost," and no one censures her. But if the man in the case indulges in such forthright language, he is a blackguard and just not nice. He can't cut through the canal here but has to go around the Horn every time. To let a girl down easy requires the utmost subtlety and resourcefulness. The main thing is, of course, to make her think it is her idea.

As we have already implied, a man must be devious, rather than direct, in extricating himself from the treacly clutches of an acquisitive female. He must provoke certain emotions, or states of mind, in her prior to his taking off. These are, in the main, indignation, boredom, and disgust; generally any one of these conditions will suffice, but one can parlay them if need be.

The first mentioned, indignation, is the quickest aroused. Sometimes a word or a remark is sufficient and the effect, if taken at the flood, may be all that is required for you to be off and running. The lavish praise of some other woman of your acquaintance or, better, the paying of undue attention to her girl friend, if she has one, may serve. Whatever the cause, the result will be the same. In her heat she will send you about your business. Taking her at her word, you will leave and be scrupulously deaf the next few days to the incessant ringing of the telephone if it is inconvenient for you to leave town. She can console herself that it was her doing and thereby keep her vanity in good repair.

ESCAPE WITH FLOWERS

Pasquale C. by collaborating with his florist, could ease himself out almost overnight by the simple act of sending a beautiful bouquet of expensive flowers (exceeding anything previously given her). In the attached sealed envelope he enclosed his card bearing an overly mushy declaration of undying love but surmounted with the name of *another* girl, all, of course, written in his own unmistakable hand. Since he found this method infallible, though expensive, he capped it with a master stroke, economically speaking. Knowing that the first female impulse upon receiving a floral tribute is to read the card, he invested in some superb facsimile flowers, tenaciously stapled in a stout cellophane wrapping, and consequently was able to use these again and again because the irate recipient of the posies invariably returned them by special messenger within the hour.

HEAVENLY BOREDOM

John N., pursuing the gentler, but more tedious, release via boredom, hatched this effective, though elaborate, disenchantment. As the young lady's prosecution of the affair vigorously waxed as his interest waned, he would extract from its hiding place a secondhand, lightweight, portable reflecting telescope and profess great enthusiasm for the study of astronomy, giving her a garbled salad of conversation laced with Flamsteed numbers, parallaxes, transits, and syzygies. He would not deign to notice her frequent yawns and fingertapping but would plunge from the obscure to the nebulous with unrelenting zeal. If talk alone didn't accomplish his ends, he would pack her off with him, telescope and all, to some draughty hilltop on a chilly, cloudless night for several hours of searching for a remote twin star scarcely visible in the two-hundred-incher at Mt. Palomar. His own instrument had a cloudy, flaking mirror that revealed nothing of interest whatsoever, providing against awakening her appetite for what might be a fascinating hobby properly pursued. Most of the time he would hog the eyepiece, exclaiming in wonder at what he saw, and then, suddenly, he would tell her to quick look at what invariably proved to be a smear of blankness. When she complained that she could see nothing, he would impatiently chide her for disturbing the focus as he elaborately readjusted the lens. He would conclude the evening, in the wee hours of the morning, by leaving her on her doorstep, chilled to the bone, while he obliviously dashed home, supposedly to report by phone to the nearest observatory about a supernova he had pretended to discover in Scorpio.

John N. found that a repeat performance was rarely necessary. A bored voice would answer his next call to inform him that she would be busy for the next week or so and would he please try some other time. He accepted this in hurt, humble tones and never called again.

To bring about the third propitious emotional state, namely disgust, we offer a C & N subterfuge which we discovered inadvertently.

BATHROOM BIT

Circuitous as this may seem, it has been known to bring

He would hog the eyepiece, exclaiming in wonder at what he saw.

about an abrupt end to an affair without making issues or having words. Leave your bathroom as it usually is without troubling to clean up the following:

> *Brush and comb with loose hair*
> *Assorted salves, ointments (labeled) for various afflictions*
> *Rings in bathtub*
> *Shower stall full of dirty laundry*
> *Old razor blades rusting in sink*
> *Used wet towels lying in water on floor*
> *Cigarette butts in soap dish*
> *Frayed toothbrush in cloudy water glass*

If the normal untidiness of the above picture is not sufficiently distressing to her because she is not fastidious herself, then add a heaping portion of these fury-rousing effects.

> *Pair of nylons on shower rail*
> *Two partially filled martini glasses containing*
> *withered olives*
> *Half-erased message in lipstick on mirror saying*
> *"Good morning, darling"*

ON YOUR WAY—OUT!

This section we consider one of our best and it is written with considerable authority.

There is that moment of surfeit in which even a Cordon Bleu plate special suddenly becomes garbage, and warmed over it is never quite the same. Somehow you will know when this happens to you, so, in spite of lame attempts on her part to conceal it, scrape yourself off and out you go. Chin up, stout fellow, and, above all, don't blubber.

You may choose to disregard the obvious signs of her new

attitude, but not for long. She will make it painfully obvious sooner or later. Whereas your slightest remark used to gain her eager attention, now, if you set yourself on fire, she wouldn't notice anything burning. What would have been a bombshell only a week before will concern her no more than the rising price of jute in the South Sea Islands. Now that you've started sprouting left feet, the better to swallow, you will discover the combined talents of Goodman Ace and S. J. Perelman couldn't get a sickly grin out of her, if you are the one giving out with the stuff.

When "dearest" becomes "dear," beware, and when your Christian name starts popping up too frequently, it is but a step to Mr. C. or Mr. N., or what are your initials anyway? The fact that she is doing none of these things deliberately but cannot help herself will make it no more palatable. When you see the handwriting on the wall and you feel the romance getting a bit drafty from her side, make the first move yourself: 1. It will be good for your morale. 2. She just might come around (but we doubt it). At best, you might gain a reprise. The main thing is not to stand upon your leaving, for, though she feels a certain tenderness on her part may be in order and that she must be gentle with you, remember that fundamentally she now regards you as a low form of life which she would rather like to kill with a stick. The idea that two people should actually be in love with each other at one and the same time is demanding too much of coincidence.

At this moment you may feel that some exhibition of indifference is required for effect. Indifference of the kind we have in mind must be assumed or put on. True indifference requires no thought, but to affect it is another matter. If you observe your girl friend closely, do not think that hers is a flawless technique, for you are observing the genuine article.

*Whereas your slightest remark used to gain her eager attention,
now if you set yourself on fire she wouldn't
notice anything burning.*

In order to show your indifference properly as you drive by
her house, keep your gaze straight ahead. This is a good idea
anyway, because, at this moment, you have undoubtedly become distraught and accident prone. We feel that passing her
house twice a day is sufficient. We do not regard it as too
feasible if she lives on a dead-end street.

You must stifle the urge to phone her. Do not seize upon
trifling excuses to call. Even legitimate reasons can be mis-
construed; for instance, after recent contretemps with a
darling little blonde, a friend of ours had suddenly decided
to collect matchbook covers and, remembering perfectly well
leaving some matches advertising Pepsi-Cola (which might
soon become collectors' items), he rang up. Needless to say,
this egocentric young lady assumed that it was merely a ruse
to talk to her; hence we advise, even in such urgent cases as
this, perhaps it is better not to call at all. It is really useless
to *show* her because, remember, she is *not* looking.

Just because what you had thought was the dalliance of
eagles turned out to be a snipe hunt, don't become too
engrossed with suffering or you will overlook a strange
advantage that may now present itself. At this moment you
have a fascination for girls who don't really interest you. Your
torch is a challenge to them and they will try to douse it for
you; they resent the fact that you think any other girl is that
desirable. This resentment works for you, but don't go on
about *her* too much or they will start to swallow the yawn,
and you will play miss-out on the ultimate commiseration
they are about to offer.

Nothing will soften your groans more surely than the
passage of time. The length of the cure varies with the tem-
perament of the afflicted. (A *graduate* bachelor can usually
recover from one of these seizures by closing his eyes and

lying down for twenty minutes.) Build up the hours spent out of contact with the cause of your grief—and—let *her* wait (you'll be amazed at her patience). It's rather like killing a turtle with a broom, we know, but you'll get over it finally.

13. Nice Girl

Unrequited love is the natural consequence of associating with nice girls. Of all the women a man may encounter, we believe the NICE GIRL to be the most dangerous. She is really the villain of this piece, hence we shall devote an entire chapter to this creature. No man is secure from her. To be her victim means either pain or matrimony (forgive our redundance), and, with the latter unpleasantness, your career as a bachelor comes to an inglorious end. She comes along like a late upstate return and upsets all your plans. She gets a ring on the finger and you get one in the nose.

We did not include the NICE GIRL in our previous classifications because she might be any one of these, or a combination of several. The name NICE GIRL itself is inadequate but, after thrashing about, we can come up with nothing better. She clouds the mind and stays the tongue. She may not be "nice" at all, but, at any rate, you will think so. And, believe it or not, she may not resemble your mother in any way.

For centuries, in fact and fiction, she has roamed rough-shod over man's affections, ignoring or setting aside the law of diminishing returns which ordinarily forestalls rashness in men's behavior. She brings with her a sickness not unlike alcoholism, for, with her, one kiss is too many and a thousand not enough. Loathe as we are to associate ourselves with moderation in any form, here we must go so far as to insist upon complete abstention.

The NICE GIRL is as deadly as a mongoose. This simpering creature can be your undoing unless recognized early. All the wiles and ways advanced in this book will not help you against this one. A dewy look, a touch of a finger tip, and everything is lost. She does not fight fairly; in fact, she doesn't fight at all. It is like trying to go ten fast rounds with a Quaker. She turns the other cheek and you, you dope, you kiss it. (What else is there to do?) You find yourself remembering her birthday, St. Valentine's Day—you start inventing holidays, in order to give her something you can't afford in exchange for something you can't have. Other girls who deny you nothing get just that in return. But this ONE!

How do you recognize her? She may not be quite as pretty as the rest (like hell she's not!!), nor as sexy (hmmmm?), but there's usually something about her eyes—they are just kind of, somehow. It's really hard to say just what she looks like. (For all we can tell, she might even look like our secretary, Miss Ampersand.[1]) The way you really know her is by the following absurd symptoms:

If holding her hand seems to be a pleasure in itself, watch out!

If you find yourself phoning her for no reason at all beware.

If you detect any desire on your part for self-improvement, heads up.

---

1 Gee, fellows, thanks a whole. Miss A.

If you begin to think you are not good enough for her, believe it, and run for the hills.

If you find yourself patting little children on their heads and loving the whole world and all that's in it, get hold of yourself, boy.

CELESTIAL PODIUMS

One of the surest signs that you have met your NICE GIRL will be your inclination to place her on a pedestal. You will do this, strangely enough, not to impress her, but yourself. Once you get her up there on that pinnacle, you will stand in rapt wonder before your own handiwork. Pedestals, as we know, are used to raise objects which lack elevation in themselves. A woman is placed there to afford a more interesting view of her, and, finding herself there, she can do nothing but look down upon you. While you may see the best aspect of her, she is enjoying the worst of you.

A certain chap close to us, Teddy H. by name, can get a girl up on a pedestal faster than a mouse can get her on a kitchen stool. Most of his pedestals, however, were of the jerry-built, collapsible type, as common as rented chairs from a funeral hall. In fact, some were so insubstantial that his whole routine was more nearly like a levitation act, and the sound of falling bodies was sometimes deafening.

Unfortunately, most men do not have the pragmatic, healthy outlook of Teddy H., for they construct their pedestals solidly and succeed in making that which was ready at hand now seem unattainable. Perhaps you have placed yourself in just such a predicament. If so, at this point, an outlandish notion may present itself to your now distraught mind. Yours is the desperation of a castaway who is ready to drink sea water. The monstrous thought occurs to you

One of the surest signs that you have met your Nice Girl will be your inclination to place her on a pedestal.

that you might win her over if you were to ask her to *marry* you! But you may be in for a rude shock. Imagine your dismay if she refuses! (You will be amazed at the number of girls who actually do not wish to marry you.) On the other hand, imagine your dismay if she accepts!

LETTER TO PUBLISHER

Dear Lee,

Sorry things seem to be moving so slowly with the manual, but we still hope to meet the deadline. Nudnick's heart just doesn't seem to be in it recently. I suspect he has not been well although he doesn't complain Yesterday, however, the results of a blood test proved negative and this seemed to buck him up no end. He feels a couple of days in Nevada should put him right as rain. He left this morning, going off in a Continental, driven by his cousin, a rather sweet looking girl who has been taking up a lot of his time recently. I couldn't help thinking they made an attractive couple.

At the moment I am looking at the back of our

Miss Ampersand's neck as she types away at the manu-
script while I scribble you this note. Things seem quiet
here without N. and, tonight, for want of anything
better to do, I shall take Miss Ampersand up on her
long standing offer to cook me a good spaghetti
dinner and meet her family. She seems like an
awfully nice girl, really.

　　　　　　　　　More later,
　　　　　　　　　　C.

NOTE FROM PUBLISHER

The above scrawl was the last we have heard from either of the two writers. After waiting patiently for some months, we have decided to publish the material on hand in what may be a vain attempt to recover what now appears to be an exorbitant advance already paid these two irresponsible nomads.

Your Little Black Book

A

NAME _____ REAL NAME _____

PET NAME _____ ADDRESS _____

PHONE NO. _____ PARTY LINE ___ PRIVATE ___

RESIDES: ALONE _____ GIRL FRIEND _____ FAMILY _____

AGE _____ ACTUAL AGE _____ BIRTH DATE _____

HEIGHT _____ HEIGHT IN HEELS _____ WEIGHT _____

WAIST _____ BUST _____ HIPS _____

BROTHER'S FIGHTING WEIGHT _____ AGE _____ DISPOSITION _____

COLOR OF EYES _____ COLOR OF HAIR _____ TRUE COLOR OF HAIR _____

STOCKING SIZE _____ SHOE SIZE _____ INSEAM MEASUREMENT _____

FAVORITE FLOWER _____ FAVORITE MUSIC _____

FAVORITE DRINK _____ FAVORITE FOOD _____

FAVORITE SEMIPRECIOUS GEM _____ FAVORITE DRIVE-IN _____

LAST TIME YOU DATED HER _____ WHERE _____

YES _____ NO _____

REMARKS _____

B

NAME _____ REAL NAME _____

PET NAME _____ ADDRESS _____

PHONE NO. _____ PARTY LINE ___ PRIVATE ___

RESIDES: ALONE _____ GIRL FRIEND _____ FAMILY _____

AGE _____ ACTUAL AGE _____ BIRTH DATE _____

HEIGHT _____ HEIGHT IN HEELS _____ WEIGHT _____

WAIST _____ BUST _____ HIPS _____

BROTHER'S FIGHTING WEIGHT _____ AGE _____ DISPOSITION _____

COLOR OF EYES _____ COLOR OF HAIR _____ TRUE COLOR OF HAIR _____

STOCKING SIZE _____ SHOE SIZE _____ INSEAM MEASUREMENT _____

FAVORITE FLOWER _____ FAVORITE MUSIC _____

FAVORITE DRINK _____ FAVORITE FOOD _____

FAVORITE SEMIPRECIOUS GEM _____ FAVORITE DRIVE-IN _____

LAST TIME YOU DATED HER _____ WHERE _____

YES _____ NO _____

REMARKS _____

e

NAME _____ REAL NAME _____

PET NAME _____ ADDRESS _____

PHONE NO. _____ PARTY LINE ___ PRIVATE ___

RESIDES: ALONE _____ GIRL FRIEND _____ FAMILY _____

AGE _____ ACTUAL AGE _____ BIRTH DATE _____

HEIGHT _____ HEIGHT IN HEELS _____ WEIGHT _____

WAIST _____ BUST _____ HIPS _____

BROTHER'S FIGHTING WEIGHT _____ AGE _____ DISPOSITION _____

COLOR OF EYES _____ COLOR OF HAIR _____ TRUE COLOR OF HAIR _____

STOCKING SIZE _____ SHOE SIZE _____ INSEAM MEASUREMENT _____

FAVORITE FLOWER _____ FAVORITE MUSIC _____

FAVORITE DRINK _____ FAVORITE FOOD _____

FAVORITE SEMIPRECIOUS GEM _____ FAVORITE DRIVE-IN _____

LAST TIME YOU DATED HER _____ WHERE _____

YES _____ NO _____

REMARKS _____

D

NAME _____ REAL NAME _____

PET NAME _____ ADDRESS _____

PHONE NO. _____ PARTY LINE ____ PRIVATE ____

RESIDES: ALONE _____ GIRL FRIEND _____ FAMILY _____

AGE _____ ACTUAL AGE _____ BIRTH DATE _____

HEIGHT _____ HEIGHT IN HEELS _____ WEIGHT _____

WAIST _____ BUST _____ HIPS _____

BROTHER'S FIGHTING WEIGHT _____ AGE _____ DISPOSITION _____

COLOR OF EYES ____ COLOR OF HAIR ____ TRUE COLOR OF HAIR ____

STOCKING SIZE _____ SHOE SIZE _____ INSEAM MEASUREMENT _____

FAVORITE FLOWER _____ FAVORITE MUSIC _____

FAVORITE DRINK _____ FAVORITE FOOD _____

FAVORITE SEMIPRECIOUS GEM _____ FAVORITE DRIVE-IN _____

LAST TIME YOU DATED HER _____ WHERE _____

YES _____ NO _____

REMARKS _____

E

NAME _____ REAL NAME _____

PET NAME _____ ADDRESS _____

PHONE NO. _____ PARTY LINE ___ PRIVATE ___

RESIDES: ALONE _____ GIRL FRIEND _____ FAMILY _____

AGE _____ ACTUAL AGE _____ BIRTH DATE _____

HEIGHT _____ HEIGHT IN HEELS _____ WEIGHT _____

WAIST _____ BUST _____ HIPS _____

BROTHER'S FIGHTING WEIGHT _____ AGE _____ DISPOSITION _____

COLOR OF EYES _____ COLOR OF HAIR _____ TRUE COLOR OF HAIR _____

STOCKING SIZE _____ SHOE SIZE _____ INSEAM MEASUREMENT _____

FAVORITE FLOWER _____ FAVORITE MUSIC _____

FAVORITE DRINK _____ FAVORITE FOOD _____

FAVORITE SEMIPRECIOUS GEM _____ FAVORITE DRIVE-IN _____

LAST TIME YOU DATED HER _____ WHERE _____

YES _____ NO _____

REMARKS _____

7

NAME _____ REAL NAME _____

PET NAME _____ ADDRESS _____

PHONE NO. _____ PARTY LINE ____ PRIVATE ____

RESIDES: ALONE _____ GIRL FRIEND _____ FAMILY _____

AGE _____ ACTUAL AGE _____ BIRTH DATE _____

HEIGHT _____ HEIGHT IN HEELS _____ WEIGHT _____

WAIST _____ BUST _____ HIPS _____

BROTHER'S FIGHTING WEIGHT _____ AGE _____ DISPOSITION _____

COLOR OF EYES _____ COLOR OF HAIR _____ TRUE COLOR OF HAIR _____

STOCKING SIZE _____ SHOE SIZE _____ INSEAM MEASUREMENT _____

FAVORITE FLOWER _____ FAVORITE MUSIC _____

FAVORITE DRINK _____ FAVORITE FOOD _____

FAVORITE SEMIPRECIOUS GEM _____ FAVORITE DRIVE-IN _____

LAST TIME YOU DATED HER _____ WHERE _____

YES _____ NO _____

REMARKS _____

g

NAME _____ REAL NAME _____

PET NAME _____ ADDRESS _____

PHONE NO. _____ PARTY LINE __ PRIVATE __

RESIDES: ALONE _____ GIRL FRIEND _____ FAMILY _____

AGE _____ ACTUAL AGE _____ BIRTH DATE _____

HEIGHT _____ HEIGHT IN HEELS _____ WEIGHT _____

WAIST _____ BUST _____ HIPS _____

BROTHER'S FIGHTING WEIGHT _____ AGE _____ DISPOSITION _____

COLOR OF EYES _____ COLOR OF HAIR _____ TRUE COLOR OF HAIR _____

STOCKING SIZE _____ SHOE SIZE _____ INSEAM MEASUREMENT _____

FAVORITE FLOWER _____ FAVORITE MUSIC _____

FAVORITE DRINK _____ FAVORITE FOOD _____

FAVORITE SEMIPRECIOUS GEM _____ FAVORITE DRIVE-IN _____

LAST TIME YOU DATED HER _____ WHERE _____

YES _____ NO _____

REMARKS _____

H

NAME _____ REAL NAME _____

PET NAME _____ ADDRESS _____

PHONE NO. _____ PARTY LINE ____ PRIVATE ____

RESIDES: ALONE _____ GIRL FRIEND _____ FAMILY _____

AGE _____ ACTUAL AGE _____ BIRTH DATE _____

HEIGHT _____ HEIGHT IN HEELS _____ WEIGHT _____

WAIST _____ BUST _____ HIPS _____

BROTHER'S FIGHTING WEIGHT _____ AGE _____ DISPOSITION _____

COLOR OF EYES _____ COLOR OF HAIR _____ TRUE COLOR OF HAIR _____

STOCKING SIZE _____ SHOE SIZE _____ INSEAM MEASUREMENT _____

FAVORITE FLOWER _____ FAVORITE MUSIC _____

FAVORITE DRINK _____ FAVORITE FOOD _____

FAVORITE SEMIPRECIOUS GEM _____ FAVORITE DRIVE-IN _____

LAST TIME YOU DATED HER _____ WHERE _____

YES _____ NO _____

REMARKS _____

7

NAME _____ REAL NAME _____

PET NAME _____ ADDRESS _____

PHONE NO. _____ PARTY LINE ___ PRIVATE ___

RESIDES: ALONE _____ GIRL FRIEND _____ FAMILY _____

AGE _____ ACTUAL AGE _____ BIRTH DATE _____

HEIGHT _____ HEIGHT IN HEELS _____ WEIGHT _____

WAIST _____ BUST _____ HIPS _____

BROTHER'S FIGHTING WEIGHT _____ AGE _____ DISPOSITION _____

COLOR OF EYES _____ COLOR OF HAIR _____ TRUE COLOR OF HAIR _____

STOCKING SIZE _____ SHOE SIZE _____ INSEAM MEASUREMENT _____

FAVORITE FLOWER _____ FAVORITE MUSIC _____

FAVORITE DRINK _____ FAVORITE FOOD _____

FAVORITE SEMIPRECIOUS GEM _____ FAVORITE DRIVE-IN _____

LAST TIME YOU DATED HER _____ WHERE _____

YES _____ NO _____

REMARKS _____

g

NAME _____ REAL NAME _____

PET NAME _____ ADDRESS _____

PHONE NO. _____ PARTY LINE ___ PRIVATE ___

RESIDES: ALONE _____ GIRL FRIEND _____ FAMILY _____

AGE _____ ACTUAL AGE _____ BIRTH DATE _____

HEIGHT _____ HEIGHT IN HEELS _____ WEIGHT _____

WAIST _____ BUST _____ HIPS _____

BROTHER'S FIGHTING WEIGHT _____ AGE _____ DISPOSITION _____

COLOR OF EYES _____ COLOR OF HAIR _____ TRUE COLOR OF HAIR _____

STOCKING SIZE _____ SHOE SIZE _____ INSEAM MEASUREMENT _____

FAVORITE FLOWER _____ FAVORITE MUSIC _____

FAVORITE DRINK _____ FAVORITE FOOD _____

FAVORITE SEMIPRECIOUS GEM _____ FAVORITE DRIVE-IN _____

LAST TIME YOU DATED HER _____ WHERE _____

YES _____ NO _____

REMARKS _____

𝒦

NAME _____ REAL NAME _____

PET NAME _____ ADDRESS _____

PHONE NO. _____ PARTY LINE ___ PRIVATE ___

RESIDES: ALONE _____ GIRL FRIEND _____ FAMILY _____

AGE _____ ACTUAL AGE _____ BIRTH DATE _____

HEIGHT _____ HEIGHT IN HEELS _____ WEIGHT _____

WAIST _____ BUST _____ HIPS _____

BROTHER'S FIGHTING WEIGHT _____ AGE _____ DISPOSITION _____

COLOR OF EYES _____ COLOR OF HAIR _____ TRUE COLOR OF HAIR _____

STOCKING SIZE _____ SHOE SIZE _____ INSEAM MEASUREMENT _____

FAVORITE FLOWER _____ FAVORITE MUSIC _____

FAVORITE DRINK _____ FAVORITE FOOD _____

FAVORITE SEMIPRECIOUS GEM _____ FAVORITE DRIVE-IN _____

LAST TIME YOU DATED HER _____ WHERE _____

YES _____ NO _____

REMARKS _____

L

NAME _____ REAL NAME _____

PET NAME _____ ADDRESS _____

PHONE NO. _____ PARTY LINE ___ PRIVATE ___

RESIDES: ALONE _____ GIRL FRIEND _____ FAMILY _____

AGE _____ ACTUAL AGE _____ BIRTH DATE _____

HEIGHT _____ HEIGHT IN HEELS _____ WEIGHT _____

WAIST _____ BUST _____ HIPS _____

BROTHER'S FIGHTING WEIGHT _____ AGE _____ DISPOSITION _____

COLOR OF EYES _____ COLOR OF HAIR _____ TRUE COLOR OF HAIR _____

STOCKING SIZE _____ SHOE SIZE _____ INSEAM MEASUREMENT _____

FAVORITE FLOWER _____ FAVORITE MUSIC _____

FAVORITE DRINK _____ FAVORITE FOOD _____

FAVORITE SEMIPRECIOUS GEM _____ FAVORITE DRIVE-IN _____

LAST TIME YOU DATED HER _____ WHERE _____

YES _____ NO _____

REMARKS _____

m

NAME _____ REAL NAME _____

PET NAME _____ ADDRESS _____

PHONE NO. _____ PARTY LINE ___ PRIVATE ___

RESIDES: ALONE _____ GIRL FRIEND _____ FAMILY _____

AGE _____ ACTUAL AGE _____ BIRTH DATE _____

HEIGHT _____ HEIGHT IN HEELS _____ WEIGHT _____

WAIST _____ BUST _____ HIPS _____

BROTHER'S FIGHTING WEIGHT _____ AGE _____ DISPOSITION _____

COLOR OF EYES _____ COLOR OF HAIR _____ TRUE COLOR OF HAIR _____

STOCKING SIZE _____ SHOE SIZE _____ INSEAM MEASUREMENT _____

FAVORITE FLOWER _____ FAVORITE MUSIC _____

FAVORITE DRINK _____ FAVORITE FOOD _____

FAVORITE SEMIPRECIOUS GEM _____ FAVORITE DRIVE-IN _____

LAST TIME YOU DATED HER _____ WHERE _____

YES _____ NO _____

REMARKS _____

n

NAME _____ REAL NAME _____

PET NAME _____ ADDRESS _____

PHONE NO. _____ PARTY LINE ___ PRIVATE ___

RESIDES: ALONE _____ GIRL FRIEND _____ FAMILY _____

AGE _____ ACTUAL AGE _____ BIRTH DATE _____

HEIGHT _____ HEIGHT IN HEELS _____ WEIGHT _____

WAIST _____ BUST _____ HIPS _____

BROTHER'S FIGHTING WEIGHT _____ AGE _____ DISPOSITION _____

COLOR OF EYES _____ COLOR OF HAIR _____ TRUE COLOR OF HAIR _____

STOCKING SIZE _____ SHOE SIZE _____ INSEAM MEASUREMENT _____

FAVORITE FLOWER _____ FAVORITE MUSIC _____

FAVORITE DRINK _____ FAVORITE FOOD _____

FAVORITE SEMIPRECIOUS GEM _____ FAVORITE DRIVE-IN _____

LAST TIME YOU DATED HER _____ WHERE _____

YES _____ NO _____

REMARKS _____

O P

NAME _____ REAL NAME _____

PET NAME _____ ADDRESS _____

PHONE NO. _____ PARTY LINE ___ PRIVATE ___

RESIDES: ALONE _____ GIRL FRIEND _____ FAMILY _____

AGE _____ ACTUAL AGE _____ BIRTH DATE _____

HEIGHT _____ HEIGHT IN HEELS _____ WEIGHT _____

WAIST _____ BUST _____ HIPS _____

BROTHER'S FIGHTING WEIGHT _____ AGE _____ DISPOSITION _____

COLOR OF EYES _____ COLOR OF HAIR _____ TRUE COLOR OF HAIR _____

STOCKING SIZE _____ SHOE SIZE _____ INSEAM MEASUREMENT _____

FAVORITE FLOWER _____ FAVORITE MUSIC _____

FAVORITE DRINK _____ FAVORITE FOOD _____

FAVORITE SEMIPRECIOUS GEM _____ FAVORITE DRIVE-IN _____

LAST TIME YOU DATED HER _____ WHERE _____

YES _____ NO _____

REMARKS _____

2 R

NAME _____ REAL NAME _____

PET NAME _____ ADDRESS _____

PHONE NO. _____ PARTY LINE ___ PRIVATE ___

RESIDES: ALONE _____ GIRL FRIEND _____ FAMILY _____

AGE _____ ACTUAL AGE _____ BIRTH DATE _____

HEIGHT _____ HEIGHT IN HEELS _____ WEIGHT _____

WAIST _____ BUST _____ HIPS _____

BROTHER'S FIGHTING WEIGHT _____ AGE _____ DISPOSITION _____

COLOR OF EYES _____ COLOR OF HAIR _____ TRUE COLOR OF HAIR _____

STOCKING SIZE _____ SHOE SIZE _____ INSEAM MEASUREMENT _____

FAVORITE FLOWER _____ FAVORITE MUSIC _____

FAVORITE DRINK _____ FAVORITE FOOD _____

FAVORITE SEMIPRECIOUS GEM _____ FAVORITE DRIVE-IN _____

LAST TIME YOU DATED HER _____ WHERE _____

YES _____ NO _____

REMARKS _____

S

NAME _____ REAL NAME _____

PET NAME _____ ADDRESS _____

PHONE NO. _____ PARTY LINE ___ PRIVATE ___

RESIDES: ALONE _____ GIRL FRIEND _____ FAMILY _____

AGE _____ ACTUAL AGE _____ BIRTH DATE _____

HEIGHT _____ HEIGHT IN HEELS _____ WEIGHT _____

WAIST _____ BUST _____ HIPS _____

BROTHER'S FIGHTING WEIGHT _____ AGE _____ DISPOSITION _____

COLOR OF EYES _____ COLOR OF HAIR _____ TRUE COLOR OF HAIR _____

STOCKING SIZE _____ SHOE SIZE _____ INSEAM MEASUREMENT _____

FAVORITE FLOWER _____ FAVORITE MUSIC _____

FAVORITE DRINK _____ FAVORITE FOOD _____

FAVORITE SEMIPRECIOUS GEM _____ FAVORITE DRIVE-IN _____

LAST TIME YOU DATED HER _____ WHERE _____

YES _____ NO _____

REMARKS _____

7

NAME _____ REAL NAME _____

PET NAME _____ ADDRESS _____

PHONE NO. _____ PARTY LINE ___ PRIVATE ___

RESIDES: ALONE _____ GIRL FRIEND _____ FAMILY _____

AGE _____ ACTUAL AGE _____ BIRTH DATE _____

HEIGHT _____ HEIGHT IN HEELS _____ WEIGHT _____

WAIST _____ BUST _____ HIPS _____

BROTHER'S FIGHTING WEIGHT _____ AGE _____ DISPOSITION _____

COLOR OF EYES _____ COLOR OF HAIR _____ TRUE COLOR OF HAIR _____

STOCKING SIZE _____ SHOE SIZE _____ INSEAM MEASUREMENT _____

FAVORITE FLOWER _____ FAVORITE MUSIC _____

FAVORITE DRINK _____ FAVORITE FOOD _____

FAVORITE SEMIPRECIOUS GEM _____ FAVORITE DRIVE-IN _____

LAST TIME YOU DATED HER _____ WHERE _____

YES _____ NO _____

REMARKS _____

U

NAME _____ REAL NAME _____

PET NAME _____ ADDRESS _____

PHONE NO. _____ PARTY LINE ___ PRIVATE ___

RESIDES: ALONE _____ GIRL FRIEND _____ FAMILY _____

AGE _____ ACTUAL AGE _____ BIRTH DATE _____

HEIGHT _____ HEIGHT IN HEELS _____ WEIGHT _____

WAIST _____ BUST _____ HIPS _____

BROTHER'S FIGHTING WEIGHT _____ AGE _____ DISPOSITION _____

COLOR OF EYES _____ COLOR OF HAIR _____ TRUE COLOR OF HAIR _____

STOCKING SIZE _____ SHOE SIZE _____ INSEAM MEASUREMENT _____

FAVORITE FLOWER _____ FAVORITE MUSIC _____

FAVORITE DRINK _____ FAVORITE FOOD _____

FAVORITE SEMIPRECIOUS GEM _____ FAVORITE DRIVE-IN _____

LAST TIME YOU DATED HER _____ WHERE _____

YES _____ NO _____

REMARKS _____

𝓥

NAME _____ REAL NAME _____

PET NAME _____ ADDRESS _____

PHONE NO. _____ PARTY LINE ____ PRIVATE ____

RESIDES: ALONE _____ GIRL FRIEND _____ FAMILY _____

AGE _____ ACTUAL AGE _____ BIRTH DATE _____

HEIGHT _____ HEIGHT IN HEELS _____ WEIGHT _____

WAIST _____ BUST _____ HIPS _____

BROTHER'S FIGHTING WEIGHT _____ AGE _____ DISPOSITION _____

COLOR OF EYES _____ COLOR OF HAIR _____ TRUE COLOR OF HAIR _____

STOCKING SIZE _____ SHOE SIZE _____ INSEAM MEASUREMENT _____

FAVORITE FLOWER _____ FAVORITE MUSIC _____

FAVORITE DRINK _____ FAVORITE FOOD _____

FAVORITE SEMIPRECIOUS GEM _____ FAVORITE DRIVE-IN _____

LAST TIME YOU DATED HER _____ WHERE _____

YES _____ NO _____

REMARKS _____

W

NAME _____ REAL NAME _____

PET NAME _____ ADDRESS _____

PHONE NO. _____ PARTY LINE ___ PRIVATE ___

RESIDES: ALONE _____ GIRL FRIEND _____ FAMILY _____

AGE _____ ACTUAL AGE _____ BIRTH DATE _____

HEIGHT _____ HEIGHT IN HEELS _____ WEIGHT _____

WAIST _____ BUST _____ HIPS _____

BROTHER'S FIGHTING WEIGHT _____ AGE _____ DISPOSITION _____

COLOR OF EYES _____ COLOR OF HAIR _____ TRUE COLOR OF HAIR _____

STOCKING SIZE _____ SHOE SIZE _____ INSEAM MEASUREMENT _____

FAVORITE FLOWER _____ FAVORITE MUSIC _____

FAVORITE DRINK _____ FAVORITE FOOD _____

FAVORITE SEMIPRECIOUS GEM _____ FAVORITE DRIVE-IN _____

LAST TIME YOU DATED HER _____ WHERE _____

YES _____ NO _____

REMARKS _____

X Y Z

NAME _____ REAL NAME _____

PET NAME _____ ADDRESS _____

PHONE NO. _____ PARTY LINE ___ PRIVATE ___

RESIDES: ALONE _____ GIRL FRIEND _____ FAMILY _____

AGE _____ ACTUAL AGE _____ BIRTH DATE _____

HEIGHT _____ HEIGHT IN HEELS _____ WEIGHT _____

WAIST _____ BUST _____ HIPS _____

BROTHER'S FIGHTING WEIGHT _____ AGE _____ DISPOSITION _____

COLOR OF EYES _____ COLOR OF HAIR _____ TRUE COLOR OF HAIR _____

STOCKING SIZE _____ SHOE SIZE _____ INSEAM MEASUREMENT _____

FAVORITE FLOWER _____ FAVORITE MUSIC _____

FAVORITE DRINK _____ FAVORITE FOOD _____

FAVORITE SEMIPRECIOUS GEM _____ FAVORITE DRIVE-IN _____

LAST TIME YOU DATED HER _____ WHERE _____

YES _____ NO _____

REMARKS _____